A Culture
of Purpose

A Culture of Purpose

HOW TO CHOOSE THE RIGHT PEOPLE AND MAKE THE RIGHT PEOPLE CHOOSE YOU

Christoph Lueneburger

Foreword by Daniel Goleman

JB JOSSEY-BASS™
A Wiley Brand

Published by Jossey-Bass
A Wiley Brand
One Montgomery Street, Suite 1200, San Francisco, CA 94104-4594
www.josseybass.com

Jossey-Bass books and products are available through most bookstores. To contact Jossey-Bass directly call our Customer Care Department within the U.S. at 800-956-7739, outside the U.S. at 317-572-3986, or fax 317-572-4002.

Wiley publishes in a variety of print and electronic formats and by print-on-demand. Some material included with standard print versions of this book may not be included in e-books or in print-on-demand. If this book refers to media such as a CD or DVD that is not included in the version you purchased, you may download this material at **http://booksupport.wiley.com**. For more information about Wiley products, visit **www.wiley.com**.

Library of Congress Cataloging-in-Publication Data

Lueneburger, Christoph, 1971-

A culture of purpose : how to choose the right people and make the right people choose you / Christoph Lueneburger.—First edition.

    pages cm

  Includes bibliographical references and index.

  ISBN 978-1-118-81456-7 (hardback); ISBN 978-1-118-89599-3 (pdf); ISBN 978-1-118-89604-4 (epub)

  1. Leadership. 2. Organizational behavior. 3. Corporate culture. I. Title.

  HD57.7.L84 2014

  658.4′092—dc23

2013050128

Printed in the United States of America
FIRST EDITION
HB Printing 10 9 8 7 6 5 4 3 2 1

To Brigitte and Anne and Liv, who give me purpose

Contents

Foreword

Daniel Goleman
Author of **Emotional Intelligence**

Today's leaders face a conundrum: our systems of transportation, energy, construction, industry, and commerce are slowly degrading the handful of systems that support life as we know it on this planet. These negative impacts are unintended—those systems were developed long before we had any idea of their ecological consequences.

Carbon and the resultant climate change are the best known of these systemic harms, but their range is far greater than dangers to the planet's carbon cycle. They include a planetwide buildup of toxic chemicals, a shrinking of biodiversity as species die off, and the acidification of bodies of water.

The human brain, unfortunately, does not attune well to these dangers to our species' long-term survival. Our brain's design for perception and for alarms of threat is attuned to the predators of an earlier age, not these subtle threats to our planet.

That leadership challenge is background to the constructs and tools Christoph Lueneburger offers here. In this leadership manifesto for the twenty-first century, he cites myriad ways managers already have risen to the challenge of making their companies' cultures ever more sustainable.

Any leader who cares about sustainability will find a practical playbook here. Let me highlight two tools.

The first: a clear, evidence-based focus on the competencies that distinguish effective sustainability leaders. The relevant leadership competencies—what to look for in new hires, promotions, and development—include the abilities to lead change and to influence. In other words, the elite in this leadership group are managers who can persuade and motivate and who articulate a resonant vision.

This provides the psychological energy and fuel that leading change demands. For creating a more sustainable system of industry and commerce will inevitably require innovations ranging from simply changing B2B sourcing to reinventing basic technologies so that they are more earth friendly.

The other competencies that distinguish the best sustainability leaders are results delivery, commercial drive, and smart strategic thinking. In other words, changes toward a more sustainable operation must also make business sense. At their best, they can go beyond saving money to creating entirely new products and processes.

The second management tool, one that goes hand in hand with this strategy, is the "handprint," the metric for all the ways an organization reduces its ecological footprint. Focusing on a company's handprint offers sustainability leaders a workaround for the adverse psychological effects of tracking carbon footprints. The footprint is always a negative value, a measure of the harm we do to the planet. This, psychologists tell us, evokes negative feelings—guilt, shame, defensiveness, and the like. These are demotivating.

But the handprint tracks the *good* we do—it's a metric for all the ways we are reducing our footprint. This is the appropriate measure for sustainability. And it makes us feel good about what we are doing. This positive motivation keeps us moving toward our goals and gives a sustainability leader a powerful tool for persuasion.

All of this makes a company's sustainability strategy the core of a culture of purpose—a set of norms and practices for the common good. As sustainable practices foster a culture of purpose, one that enlarges its handprint daily, companies can better attract and retain the best talent among those generations that will bear the brunt of our past poor ecological habits. And having the best and brightest will help any company both in its immediate results and in its long-term battle to reverse the ecological tide.

Although the ecological crisis we face as a species can seem gloomy, I find great hope in the case studies presented here. To see the range of ideas, innovations, and more sustainable practices already promoted by leaders suggests that we are at the dawn of a new way of doing business—one with a realistic sense of how culture matters for the long term and an intelligent grasp of how a more sustainable mode can be good strategy.

Following this map, perhaps one day industry and commerce will go beyond sustainability to replenishing the earth.

Introduction

What is the most important challenge for a twenty-first-century leader?

Building a culture of purpose.

Cultures of purpose power winning organizations. And although leaders are right to track innovation, differentiation, and profitability, it is in cultures of purpose that any of these last.

Cultures of purpose don't fall from the sky; they don't spring from happy accidents or baffling evolutions. Such cultures are built, over time and with concrete building blocks. Sustainability provides the most reliable blueprint for assembling these building blocks into a culture of purpose.

As words go, *sustainability* is about as evocative as elevator Muzak. Both vague and ubiquitous, the term has been so overused that it means everything and nothing. But when the elevator stops, so does the Muzak, and what remains of sustainability is the answer to the key question leaders ask: *How do I get the smartest, most creative and passionate people to come help my organization navigate challenges and exploit future opportunities that are only faintly visible to me?*

1

Sustainability, therefore, is not a description of a set of problems. It's a solution to them. It forges cultures and inspires consumers. And where it connects with the purpose of your organization, it attracts the most passionate hearts and the most creative minds, who will flock to you because there is no place they'd rather be. That is why "being sustainable" is a statement about your organization rather than about trees or solar power. It's also why sustainability is a way of doing business that builds cultures of purpose.

What is a culture of purpose? Let's start with the *culture* itself: a set of beliefs and customs, the kinds of thinking and behaving that define an organization.[1] It's "the way things work around here," the air we breathe.

Now add *purpose*. Aspirational but actionable, purpose introduces a shared intent with impact beyond the organization itself. Because it captures an ideal, a purpose goes beyond profitable growth, shareholder value, or any other measure of whether you are doing things right. A purpose, instead, is a pledge to *do the right things*. Audacious and bold, a purpose inspires a meaningful number of people to take action.

Why am I writing about cultures of purpose? I am a partner at Egon Zehnder, a global leader in matching talent and strategy. With sixty-eight offices around the world, Egon Zehnder partners with companies, nonprofits, and governments in appraising their current leaders, finding new ones, and assessing their collective effectiveness at both the executive and the board levels. Since I founded the Sustainability Practice at Egon Zehnder, we have partnered with clients on well over six hundred sustainability assignments globally. This book captures the key lesson

2

of that journey: how to build a culture of purpose by embracing sustainability as a commercial theme.

In my work, I deconstruct cultures of purpose into three sets of building blocks: competencies, traits, and cultural attributes. Let's spend a moment on each of these.

Competencies are quantifiable characteristics of a person that differentiate performance in a specific role. Put simply, they predict who is good at a particular job. People selected for roles using competency-based assessment perform significantly better than those who are not, and they tend to stay with the organization significantly longer.[2] Not surprisingly, the more senior the role, the bigger the impact of small differences in competencies. For this reason, I will use competencies to describe the core of the organization: its leaders.

Like muscles in a body, competencies can be cultivated over time. Because they can be taught and learned, your opportunity as a leader is to ensure not only that others develop them but also that you do. Your actions—selecting the right leaders according to their competencies so as to shape the core of your organization—have an immediate impact on your culture.

The competencies differentiating leaders in a culture of purpose are *change leadership, influencing, results delivery, commercial drive*, and *strategic orientation*.

Next up are *traits*. These are innate personality elements that describe the ability of a person to grow and to handle responsibilities of greater scale and scope. Put simply, traits are predictive markers for future development and success. To change one's traits requires real conviction and massive effort: unlike competencies, they cannot be taught or learned, but they *can* be assessed and fostered.

Traits provide a lens through which to gauge individuals anywhere in your company, some of whom will converge from the frontier—the showrooms and store aisles, the factory floors and client lobbies—toward the core of the organization to become future leaders. I will therefore use traits to describe the people throughout your organization. Your opportunity as a leader is to ensure that new people joining at the frontier, whatever their level and function, possess the traits—the right raw ingredients—to help you build a culture of purpose. The impact of selecting for traits as you hire future talent builds gradually from the frontier of your business, where much of the real innovation takes place.

The individual traits essential to a culture of purpose are *engagement*, *determination*, *insight*, and *curiosity*.

Together, the core and the frontier define the boundaries of your organization. Encapsulating both and everything in between is my third vantage point: *cultural attributes*. It is not enough for people at the frontier of your organization to bring the right traits and for the leaders at its core to be competent. No matter how good the person, no matter how influential the role, the gap between reality and aspiration is rarely bridged solely by putting somebody into the right position. Individuals point the way, but cultural attributes determine whether the organization is ready to embark on the journey.

Unlike competencies and traits, cultural attributes do not pertain to individuals, but rather describe the behavior of the collective whole. Much as great players don't automatically make for a winning team (and some teams have become great without star talent), people with the right competencies and traits don't spontaneously coalesce into a culture of purpose.

As a leader, you must create an environment that unleashes these competencies and traits and pushes them to the fore. That means influencing the culture as a whole, shaping how people relate to one another and collectively gun for what would be out of reach to them individually.

The cultural attributes at the core of a culture of purpose are *energy*, *resilience*, and *openness*.

Because cultures are made up of people—and each shapes the other, from the core to the frontier—the three sets of building blocks depend on and influence each other.

More concretely, leadership competencies are enabled by individual traits. A person strongly displaying the traits of engagement and curiosity, for instance, is likely to develop a high level of the competency that these two traits enable: influencing. If the person has not already developed that competency (perhaps she is too young, or her prior roles might not have required her to influence anybody), the presence of the underlying traits tells us that she will most probably be able to do so in the future.

Individual traits exist in balance with cultural attributes. Indeed, there is a symbiosis between top talent and cultures of purpose: more than ever, the smartest and most creative minds are drawn to places that reflect their values. Individuals displaying high levels of engagement at the traits level, for example, are disproportionally drawn to high-energy cultures that allow them to express that trait, not suppress it.

This figure illustrates the interrelationships among leadership competencies, individual traits, and cultural attributes.

The Weave of Competencies, Traits and Attributes

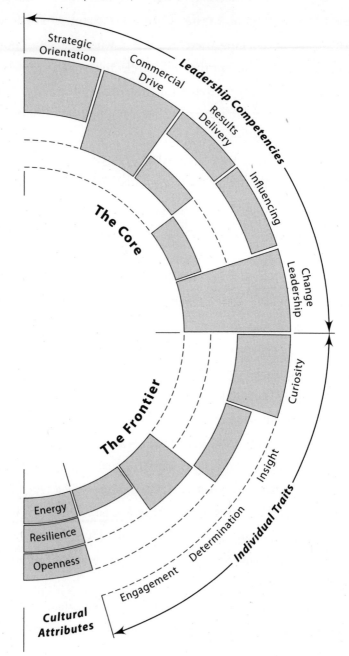

All three—competencies, traits, and cultural attributes—
are necessary building blocks for a culture of purpose. In this
book, we'll look at each of them and delve into what they mean,
how they are manifested, and what leaders can do to build, support, and harness them.

To do so, I will introduce you to a quantitative and actionable model for building a culture of purpose. As is true of any
model, it matters what went into it. Our work in sustainability
alone has allowed us to assess thousands of executives in this
sector, in settings ranging from management appraisal and culture assessments to searches for executives (from heads of sustainability to CEOs) and nonexecutives (from advisors to board
directors). Beyond work specific to sustainability, we have as a
firm conducted more than thirty-two thousand in-depth management appraisals, from line managers to CEOs, which allows
us to compare what we have learned in sustainability to the
general talent universe. We therefore understand the competencies, traits, and cultural attributes that most frequently spike
in cultures of purpose.

Fine books have been written about the "what," the "why,"
and the "how" of sustainability—about strategies and processes
and initiatives. This is a book about the "who" and the "where":
Who is needed to build cultures of purpose? Where will great
talent want to apply itself as sustainability becomes a concrete
way of traveling rather than a vague destination? Along the way,
I will show why sustainability is the most effective path to building cultures of purpose.

My connection to these questions is personal. I was ten
years old when my father came home from prison, and I did

not understand why he had been gone for so many years. In the 1980s, Germany was a country divided in conflict between socialism and capitalism, as was Europe and, for that matter, the rest of the world. My father, an engineer in East Germany, had lost faith in the system, or perhaps admitted to himself that he'd never had it. He tried to escape across the border to West Germany and was unlucky to get caught. But he was lucky not to get shot, and was sentenced to hard labor.

I was too young to understand the difference between Keynes and Marx, but I certainly sensed that we lived in an opaque world—a world in which what was said in the company of friends behind closed doors was different from what was proclaimed in public, a world in which "the system" ruled supreme. It was a culture without a purpose other than to promote the privileges of a select few, and it was not sustainable.

Ultimately, my family—rowdy objectors all—was coughed out of the system, and set about putting the greatest possible distance between itself and the communist ideology. By the time the Berlin Wall came down, we lived in the United States.

It may seem like a strange place to start a book on culture and sustainability as a path to value creation in the twenty-first century, but as I look out across Park Avenue now, I cannot think of a better historical parallel than the collapse of the Eastern Bloc to how massively and irreversibly sustainability has already begun to affect the way we live.[3] Much as the fall of communism gave voice and choice to millions of people, the rise of sustainability is enabling people to vote, at the point of purchase, for products reflective of the buyers' values. Both transitions herald spectacular discontinuities not only for the masses but also for the institutions in their midst. Just as governments tumbled and new parties arose under the banner of transparency, or "glasnost," today the imperative of transparency provides fertile ground for some companies as it buries others.

The time has never been more critical for leaders to focus on building cultures of purpose. We now know that mission-led companies vastly outperform the market.[4] We have learned that the war for talent is real. The past decade, moreover, has taught us a great deal about the systemic issues at the core of sustainable business. We therefore understand, more than ever before, the vast array of tools at our disposal to address those issues, and we have the means to use them. What we do not have enough of is, on the one hand, the leadership to act on our understanding and, on the other, the cultures to scale our action.

But we are ready for both. For this book, I interviewed chief sustainability officers, CEOs, and board chairmen.[5] (Unless otherwise noted, all quotations in the book are from these interviews.) All of them, without exception, had come to the conclusion that sustainability is a primary focus of new recruits. The topic surfaces more than any other in interviews and recruiting sessions, because the best minds of our time are looking not just for jobs but for meaning.

These are talented folks who want to be deeply invested in the long-term success of their world and the institutions which make that success possible. They don't want window-dressing policies about composting and charitable giving. They *do* want to see the meaning in their work all around them, from the C-suite to the break room. More than ever, top talent is gravitating to cultures of purpose. And therefore, in the war for talent, cultures of purpose are winning.

Here is how to build them.

PART
1

Placing Leaders with a Purpose at the Core

Culture and sustainability are products of leadership. And the impact of leaders is bounded by their competencies and the competencies of others they put in charge. In this part of the book, I will identify the competencies—or acquired skills—at the core of a culture of purpose.

The competencies discussed in the following chapters differentiate leaders who have successfully commercialized sustainability from other leaders of similar seniority and influence. Therefore, I do not here devote time to other competencies, such as team leadership, that—although important—occur equally strongly in both groups.

Competencies can be developed over time, whether through apprenticeship or sheer will. You can learn about somebody's competencies by asking *how* she did something and keeping at it until you find what she herself did, exactly, and what might have been done by others around her. In the case of the ability to influence, somebody might say, "I found out that Jack is not very focused on his economic gain, but he cares a great deal about thought leadership. So I won him over with the sheer amount of patents he was likely to generate if he were to join my project." Interesting! How did you find out about Jack—did you go out of your way to understand his modus operandi, or did somebody just happen to tell you? And how did you sell him on the trove of patents—did you have data, or did you lead with an emotive story?

You get the point: by asking behavioral "how" questions, you can find out, accurately, how well developed a particular competency is.

The Boost of Change Leadership

When Captain David Marquet took command of a Navy submarine for the first time in 1999, it was both a dream come true and a leadership nightmare. David had always wanted to be a submarine captain. He graduated near the top of his class at the U.S. Naval Academy. He trained for a year to take the helm at the USS *Olympia*. But at the very last moment, he was instead assigned to take the command of the USS *Santa Fe*, a much newer and faster ship, but also a ship with the worst performance track record in the Navy. In his first stint as a submarine captain, David found himself leading a vessel about which he knew nothing.

Taking his command, he discovered another problem: he noticed that people blindly followed directions from above and blamed "them" if the result fell short of the objective. This problem hit home one day when David gave a command ("two-thirds ahead") that—unlike on the *Olympia*—was technically impossible to execute on the *Santa Fe*. The command was relayed forward by David's senior officer, but stalled when the helmsman sheepishly informed his captain that there was no "two-thirds" on the *Santa Fe*. When David asked his senior officer if he was aware of this fact, the response was, "Yes, but you gave the order."

It was high time for a change.

That evening, David gathered his officers and told them, "Unless you start announcing your intent rather than blindly repeating orders, this submarine is simply going to drive in a straight line." David added, "In fact, I am not going to give orders." He also abolished the word "they," asking his people to instead say "we."

What changed? Everything. David's team of 135 sailors began—first with skepticism and then with commitment—to assume ownership, think about what they were doing, and strive for excellence rather than the mere avoidance of mistakes. Within a year, the crew went from the worst performing in the U.S. submarine fleet to the best, winning awards for performance and effectiveness while drastically increasing retention. Indeed, David had such lasting influence that the ship continued to win awards long after he moved on to new assignments. "The trick is not to think yourself into a different way of acting," David told me, "but to act yourself into a different way of thinking."[1]

David was unambiguously in charge of his ship, and he saw a need for change. He drove the change with purpose, and built a fundamentally different culture in doing so: one of performance and accountability. What he learned along the way was that everybody—literally everybody—can take ownership of his or her area of expertise. And when he or she is allowed to do so, "the goodness is no longer tied to you as a person; it is tied to people and what they do." The goodness, in other words, is tied to the culture. This is change leadership at work.

Change Leadership

Change leadership is about transforming and aligning an organization through its people to drive for improvement in a new and challenging direction. This competency creates a wave of change that allows any one person to have impact beyond his or her individual remit. Change leadership is not just about identifying necessary changes personally. It is possible, in fact, for someone to be a reasonably effective change leader without being a strategist. This competency is about driving change through the organization, getting others to want to change, and encouraging them to innovate themselves. What's more, it is not about forcing change on people but rather getting them on board and cultivating their willingness to accept, drive, and lead change. A critical element is the ability to engage people so that they *want* to change. And as we'll see in Chapter Six, engaging people means making them feel different about the need for change. It means finding something they truly care about.

An individual with a low level of the change leadership competency is someone who tends to think of the status quo as effective. This person may fail to see the need for change, but could still accept it if pressed. Others with low levels of this competency may accept that change is normal and think well of it in general terms—but not be eager or proactive around the topic. An individual with midlevel competency in change leadership is one who begins to actively challenge the status quo, pointing out what needs to change—though not how—and tries to help people who are struggling with this concept. This person may also define a positive direction for change and make a case others can buy into, using logic to persuade people.

Those who have a highly developed change leadership competency actively promote change with an array of approaches to start mobilizing individuals to change. They build coalitions, foster diversity of thought, coordinate the change effort across multiple individuals, and take a more long-term, sophisticated approach to introducing change. They create champions who will mobilize others to change, ultimately creating organization-wide momentum around change. Those at the highest level of this competency cultivate this quality of change across highly complex organizations, or create a culture capable of constant change for improved results.

Change leadership is a critical competency at the early stage of sustainability transformation because it is so vital in building the momentum needed to get going. Owens Corning and its chief sustainability officer, Frank O'Brien-Bernini, provide a rich case study of this competency in action.

How Frank Rejuvenated Owens Corning

Frank O'Brien-Bernini remembers the moment he began his evolution in becoming a change leader. Standing in the office of his CEO, talking to the boss about the general need to embrace sustainability issues, something in the air shifted.

16

In fact, Frank recalls, there may not have been any pronouncements made. "It was very short and sweet, led by the CEO's body language at that meeting. It was: OK, I've got it. I don't understand it, but I hear what you are saying and I trust that this is important." It was unspoken but understood. Frank knew he had his marching orders.

With that, Frank both headed the company's R&D function and became its chief sustainability officer, even though no one had really clarified what that second title entailed. At the time, Owens Corning was operating under bankruptcy protection, so sustainability meant more than the traditional "green" efforts. The very sustainability of the organization itself was on the line. Would Owens Corning emerge a viable business concern? Would it be a healthy, thriving organization in the future? Could it be, in this very stark business sense, sustainable? Frank believed that the "green" sustainability and the business sustainability goals were necessarily and uniquely intertwined. One would open the door to the other.

Frank decided that to drive change, he needed muscle. From all corners of the company, he tapped individuals to serve on the company's first Sustainability Council. The members came from different divisions, critical functions, and different places on the hierarchy; notably, they did not share any one vision for the definition of sustainability. What they did share was organizational respect and influence: they were people who could get things done. This was a key decision by Frank. He didn't want a council full of tree-huggers. Instead, he wanted a diversity of opinion as to how sustainability should play out in a manufacturing environment. It was a challenging collection of individuals, not all of whom were willing. Frank recalls, "I had one person come to me and ask, 'Why am I here? I don't need to be here.'" But if the council was to fulfill its role as part of the change process, that person did need to be there. The initial council was made up of a select cross-functional subset of the organization's most influential business leaders—typical of the lean structure of the best newly minted sustainability teams.

Frank's first task was to help the council understand its mandate. There was plenty of debate around the table during those early meetings, he recalled. "When we would get together, it was a learning thing. Few knew what it was all about." Many had questions like, "What is sustainability? Why does it matter? What is our role? Do our customers, employees, investors care? And the ultimate and potentially disempowering question: is our top leadership really committed to this?"

This kind of debate is not an uncommon or even undesirable part of a company's transformation process. In fact, it's essential as any organization moves along the sustainability continuum in pursuit of a culture of purpose. But it is also a bit of a danger zone because too often, this lack of concrete vision is used to stop the transformation before it starts. Because the team is infused with a sense of urgency but not yet armed with a road map, naysayers may take the opportunity to disparage and discourage. It's critical to remember that this urgency-without-clarity is a common, even necessary and useful emotional state. If properly channeled rather than shut down, this energy will inspire the next steps.

This is precisely how Frank dealt with his council. He told them, You are the voice of sustainability as it leaves this room and travels back into the everyday operations of this company. You are the person who will raise the sustainability issues and opportunities that matter in your space. If there is an IT project being reviewed, the IT member of this team would be the one to raise the issues of where servers are being housed and if they are more or less efficient than the servers being replaced. If you are in manufacturing, you are the voice in the meeting asking whether the latest capital project is better or worse for our environmental footprint in the plant. If you are in product development, you are the one who asks whether the new product will be better or worse than the old product when used by a customer designing to one of the various green building programs, or comparatively better than alternate solutions across its life cycle. The council, he explained, is designed not to convene and discuss its issues at one meeting, but to converge and then disseminate the need for change throughout the company.

Indeed, this is the key way in which change leadership differs from another familiar process, change advocacy. Many who have dealt with issues of sustainability are accustomed to hearing from advocates—evangelists who will come into a company or into a conference room and exhort and lecture about their brand of change. That's not unique to sustainability, of course. Change advocates preach for gun rights and for gun control; for evolution and for creationism; any cause will do, really. They favor monologue over dialogue, however. Change *leadership* augments this approach. It starts with the willingness to stand up for a point of view that requires action in close quarters, even if you are the only one in the room advocating for that particular thing (indeed especially then). Leading change means not only presenting your view to others but also transforming those people into multipliers of the message from their own vantage points.

I liken the difference between change advocacy and change leadership to the difference between a trebuchet catapult and a Trojan horse: one is designed to overcome and destroy walls, the other to be invited in. And in this invitation, I have found again and again, the seeds for a far different outcome. An individual may be swayed by a powerful lecture. But how much more impact that same message might have if it came from inside that individual's work team. Frank didn't send his team out to give lectures, but rather to convey aligned messaging and drive different actions from inside the walls of Owens Corning's culture.

Of course, not everything can be moved forward through discussion, so the council also adopted some more concrete tactics. One was the creation of a capital fund—sort of an in-house venture capital project—set to support sustainability projects around the company. "If we just go around saying, 'We are really worried about energy, and we need your help and let's all invest,' that's not going to be successful," Frank says. The council needed more firepower. It needed a way to get inside the capital investment decisions of managers all over Owens Corning. The result: a pool of funds earmarked for sustainability initiatives, with the sustainability council as its keeper and investor. Owens Corning employees, and their facilities, had an opportunity to compete for it—putting forth their best projects in hopes of securing funding. What was different here was that, over time, confidence grew that the best energy projects would get done. The extra effort to develop those projects, on the part of otherwise busy people, would absolutely be rewarded with funding.

Around the company, eager participants stepped up.

"What we ended up with was an awesome pipeline of projects—lighting projects, compressor upgrades, motor replacements, natural gas leak detection. All of these were relatively small as single projects, but had a large impact when shared across the company. We later came to call these low cost/no cost capital projects," Frank says.

At some locations, plant "green teams" sought funding to install more-efficient motion-sensing lighting in warehouses, and other off-the-shelf energy savers. Other projects were more creative. At a plant in Toronto, a particularly active plant "green team" crafted a plan for a solar wall. Their vision: paint the south wall of the building black, with a special glaze, and use that as part of the plant's space-heating system.

The projects themselves were beneficial, but their existence did much more than create small sustainability inroads throughout the company. Over time, they began to create a behavior—indeed a culture—biased toward productivity programs that reduce resource consumption.

Also as part of this change leadership process, Frank and his council began working to create a new language that supported the cultural changes of sustainability. For example, the word "broken" came to mean more than "no longer works." In a manufacturing setting, anybody would say he already knows what the word "broken" means. It means you flip the On switch and the thing doesn't work. But as part of the transformation process, the sustainability council encouraged a new definition of "broken." Now, they said, it takes on a broader meaning. Something that still functions—a fixed-speed fan, for example—is deemed broken if its efficiency is 70 percent when equipment achieving 90 percent is readily available, such as a variable-speed fan. This kind of easy and accessible language empowered people throughout the organization to look for what's broken, what could be improved.

Through his experiences, Frank learned an important truth about how to be a successful change leader. The key, he says, is to know where the task starts and finishes. Change leadership is a competency that spikes at a certain point on the journey toward sustainability—the early part. Great change leaders do their best work there, and then move on. The role, Frank says, is to give birth to the new process—in a single team or in a division or even company-wide—and once it becomes autonomous, look for the next challenge. "If you're an optimizer, this would drive you nuts," he says. "You have to hand it off well before it's optimized. You've got to love to start something and then say, OK, this team's got it, they'll improve it incrementally. And you'll move on. So you have to force yourself to stand back and let go when things are becoming most interesting, and move on to the next thing you want to ignite."

Here we see Frank, notwithstanding his C-suite title, enabling others to take ownership. Of the psychological studies that have explored how power can influence behavior, one involving cookies memorably concluded that "high-power individuals were more likely to chew with their mouths open and to get crumbs on their faces and on the table."[2] Unlike Frank, in other words, some people endowed with the power of leadership positions tend to domineer and lose consideration for others (and as we will see in the next chapter on influencing, this limits the scope of change in an organization). You might say that cookie monsters are poor change leaders, because they do not willingly share their power with others. Great change leaders, in contrast, allow those around them to take ownership, rather than monopolizing the change.

To wit, Frank decided that he'd know it was all working when the news of some sustainability success got back to him—and it was the first he'd heard of it. Frank recalls picking up the phone one day and hearing about a successful water reduction program at one of the Owens Corning plants. The caller was delivering congratulations to the chief sustainability officer, but Frank had not known about that particular effort. His knee-jerk reaction might have been, *Oh, I should have known.* But in reality, that he didn't know and that it happened without him are even more remarkable—and even more worthy of congratulations. On a day like that, when the sustainability goal was met with no input from the change leader, he could say, We've made our goals so clear and they've been embraced so completely that people take it upon themselves to do something. It may be the work of a plant supervisor or one of the environmental leaders at a division, but it's not the original sustainability council giving orders. Sustainability has become an organic part of the way the organization functions. It is change that no longer relies on a leader, because it is part of the culture.

Another sign: when the culture of purpose is so ingrained in the company that it starts to spread the message outward to customers and vendors. Frank related a story to me about a homebuilder in Denver with a strong interest in incorporating better energy efficiency into the houses he builds. Frank and his team, in partnership with the builder, have been working through a totally new approach to this process, looking for ways not only to improve energy efficiency but also to better communicate this improved performance to the home buyers: What language can be used to do essentially what was done so well at Owens Corning? How can the Denver homebuilder act as a change leader, bringing in Owens Corning as a critical part of his "sustainability council" and ultimately influencing homebuyers to want to join in the change process? It's an exciting extension of Frank's change leadership abilities, and it reflects the broader possibilities of sustainability trans-formation. Such a transformation is portable beyond your factory walls and can travel with you as you do business out in the world.

Going for the Handprint Instead of the Footprint

In addition to understanding the tactical steps of change lead-ership, it pays also to consider the tone of communications. In sustainability circles, the discussion will increasingly be framed with the "handprint" versus the "footprint" labels. Many who have heard about sustainability issues over the years are

24

familiar with the use of the word "footprint" in this context. We are constantly exhorted to reduce our footprint—that is, reduce our impact on the world around us. This is how we have been schooled to demonstrate our care for the planet and for the cause of sustainability. And it's about as motivating as daily beatings.

When it comes to change leadership, we should place our bets on handprints. Instead of focusing on reducing bad unintended consequences, let's talk about maximizing the positive impact we can actively pursue as a primary objective. Convey your information in a context of what can be done *beneficially* rather than in the negative context of what has to stop. This thinking will take you to the core of what your organization does—its purpose. And rest assured, the purpose of your organization is not to reduce carbon emissions.

In the case of Owens Corning, the footprint perspective leads you to reducing the energy footprint ever more, first relatively with respect to production and then absolutely. Ultimately, you will "win" when you shut down the business and consume no more energy. That does not sustain the business.

From the handprint perspective, in contrast, change goals consider how the world is affected by Owens Corning products—how much energy is saved in an insulated building, for example. It is a much more aspirational approach: whereas the best you can do with a footprint is get to zero, a positive handprint has no upper limit. When you frame sustainability issues in this handprint context as Frank does, you adopt a tone of aspiration and collaboration rather than criticize your listener's destructive behavior. Changing to good is much more rewarding than changing from bad. When the handprint context augments the footprint context, it is inspirational and creates a change momentum of its own.

Next

What happened to Owens Corning? When Frank began his work on sustainable change and his efforts at change leadership, the very existence of the company was on the line. Bankruptcy is a last resort and comes with considerable risks. Fix this situation by this date, or we break this company up and sell off its parts, and you fade into business history.

After six years, Owens Corning successfully emerged from bankruptcy. It emerged because it did a lot of things right and repositioned for the long term. Sustainability was an important part of that strategy and will continue to be going forward.

■ ■ ■

As we have seen with Frank's example, change leadership first requires a perspective on the need for change itself—as evidenced by the fact that nobody knew what his new title entailed. Frank believed that sustainability would be instrumental to Owens Corning's future, and he stood up for this point of view. Second, he encouraged change in individuals, starting with the council he handpicked according to members' ability to multiply the message rather than their ideology. And third, Frank scaled the change through supportive infrastructure, not only internally through the in-house capital fund that allowed everybody to participate but also externally by partnering directly with homebuilders.

Notice that Frank did not pull rank—indeed, he defines success as the process running without his prodding. Anybody can give orders. But who can lead change?

Discovering the Leader: Markers for the Competency of Change Leadership

When evaluating a potential leader, what can you look for that will tell you how this person will step up as an agent of change? The competencies of the leaders you enable to lead change will define the quality of the change itself. The incidence of highly competent change leaders at the C-level (1 in 16) is triple that of the general management population (1 in 47), and whether in a nuclear submarine or an advanced materials manufacturer, these are the people you want to put in position next to you as you drive change.

Because change leaders can be division heads, or managers of teams, or the individual in the department who can be most relied on to create forward momentum on any given project, the markers will vary widely. What follows is a list of questions to help you zero in on the ability to lead change.

What to Look For	How to Look for It
These individuals invite the most powerful people to their side—especially if they don't readily agree with them.	When have you tried to assemble a diverse group of influential people together to deliver a major change? How did you do that, and what happened?
	What person have you partnered with who was most diametrically opposed to your views? How?
By crafting narratives that reflect the personal aspirations of others, they allow others to own and feel good about change.	[Listen]
They are effective at scaling initiatives and stand back as soon as others take ownership.	When have you recruited others to become change agents?
	How did you choose and entice them?
	How do you know when to let them run with things?
They stand up for and are authentically committed to change.	When have you championed the need for change in front of a skeptical or hostile audience? How did you go about it?
	How is your devotion to this initiative reflected in your life more broadly?
They believe in the power of groups and opt to join them.	Have you played a team sport? Was there a moment when you had to help the team adopt a different point of view?
They create mechanisms that scale change through multiple degrees of separation.	How have you used social media to advance an issue?
	Tell me about a time you picked up the echo of an initiative you launched from an unexpected place.
They exploit language to build a vocabulary that captures meaning in ways bespoke to their culture.	Are there acronyms or rallying cries you have used along the way? How did they come to be? How did you use them?
	When have you found language to be at its most powerful in driving change?

28

What to Look For	How to Look for It
Favoring scale and pace over efficiency and control, they resist the temptation to optimize.	When have you handed control over to others too early? How did you pick that moment? Looking back, when could you have handed control over to others earlier? What was the opportunity cost of not doing so?

Red Flags: The opposite of change leadership is change resistance, so beware of people who consistently fail to support new business initiatives by others or to contribute meaningful ones of their own. Such individuals will generally not recognize or acknowledge any need for improvement. In referencing them, you are likely to hear frustration from those who feel that this kind of person actively resisted change even in the face of compelling evidence.

The Power of Influencing

When Antanas Mockus was elected mayor of Bogotá, Colombia, in 1995, he had no previous political experience. He took the helm of a city plagued by problems: paralyzing water shortages, dangerous traffic, and a pervasive absence of order. What could an individual person without a political network do in the face of this challenge?

Realizing that he could not rule by fiat, Antanas took an entirely different approach to his leadership challenge. He sought change not through power but through influence.

A former university math professor and the ex-president of the Colombian national university, Antanas treated Bogotá as his five-million-student classroom. A man who had once mooned a classroom full of rowdy students to get their attention (it worked), Antanas was not afraid to try the unusual. He appeared on TV while taking a shower, turning off the water as he soaped. Within a couple of months, water usage had dropped by one-seventh, and kept on dropping as economic incentives he had set up kicked in. To combat traffic woes, Antanas backed off from the ineffective policy of having police issue tickets and instead hired twenty mimes. These actors went out into the streets of the city and silently ridiculed reckless drivers and pedestrians alike, often to cheering onlookers. Public shame proved enormously effective, and Antanas hired four hundred additional mimes. Traffic fatalities fell by half during his administration.

Perhaps not surprisingly for such an effective influencer, Antanas told me, "I don't like the word *leader*. These successes were about collective leadership, and many others deserve credit." Also not surprisingly, Antanas took to wearing a Superman costume and declared himself "Super Citizen" as he kept pushing Bogotá forward through personal example and social contract.

Influencing

When presented with a problem that he did not feel belonged to him, a colleague I knew was fond of a saying: "There are two kinds of problems: My problems, and not-my-problems. What you are talking about is not my problem. Figure it out." This was fairly effective for him, but there's an alternative to his approach—indeed, the direct opposite—that can be powerful when leading transformational change in an organization. It requires embracing the problems of others. For those who seek to be effective influencers, the problems of others, their challenges and aspirations, are pay dirt. I *want* to know what keeps you up at night, because if I do, I will understand how it relates to what keeps me up at night. And where those two intersect, I can likely influence you to help me out.

Influencing is about working well with others who do not work for you, working as a team to have a positive impact on business performance. A person operating with a low level of this competency simply helps if asked and supports people when required. At a moderate level, the competency is about being a genuine team player and an effective influencer of others to get things done. People with high levels of the influencing competency proactively create partnerships and effective working teams where none existed before, on a broad or even an international scale. Importantly, higher-level influencers are able to go one step further by actively supporting and collaborating with those they have influenced, so as to yield tangible results.

Among the seventeen thousand executives we have assessed in detail, high-level influencers are nearly as common in the general management population (about 1 in 68) as they are at the C-level (1 in 40). That is an unusually small difference between the two populations and reflects the degree to which hierarchy typically drives top-down decision making. Moreover, that there are four times as many C-level executives who have *low* levels of this competency compared to the number with high levels reveals the untapped potential of influencing in the context of building cultures of purpose.

Examples of great influencing are all around us. Remember Tom Sawyer whitewashing Aunt Polly's fence and convincing his friends to do the work for him? Great influencing! This competency enables people to draw on the power and motivation of the group to energize an organization and drive change. The best and most visionary of orders fall flat and fail to inspire action when they are not anchored in the emotions and aspirations of those tasked with executing them. In a culture of purpose, great new ideas come from anywhere. Often they come from people who have no or limited formal authority to give orders to those most crucial to their realization. The ability to influence others is the lifeblood of such ideas.

Influencing is a competency we see again and again at unusually strong levels in leaders who are successful in pursuing sustainability as a commercial theme. Those who display this competency are effective in working with peers, partners, and others who are not in the line of command to have a positive impact on business performance. These are the people willing to shower on TV to influence better water conservation, or to hire mimes if that's what it takes to shame the public into better, safer driving habits. They are the leaders who understand what emotional strings to pull in order to inspire not only approval but also following and participation from various people. They will ask themselves, *How can I get the engineer with an advanced degree in finite element analysis and a passion for organic legumes and the accountant who happens to speak Farsi to do together what neither could do alone?*

The beauty of influencing is that it can be executed on both small and grand scales. Antanas Mockus sought to influence the five million of Bogotá—an ambitiously large group with which to establish a collaborative process. But leaders may also find success in much more targeted efforts. A manager within a division of twenty thousand may have limited ability to influence the full complement. But she can influence ten—those with the ability to become multipliers and vectors to carry the message out into the wider ranks. Even an individual without direct reports but a set of peers can undertake this effort, bringing along his colleagues as collaborators.

Let's look more closely at one leader's influencing journey.

How Pascal Embedded His Vision at Lend Lease

When Pascal Mittermaier first came to Lend Lease, he had no intention of using humor or any other emotional theme to make his case for sustainability. Entering the multinational construction firm in London as head of sustainability, he set out to frame the topic as an unambiguously commercial one. He had come from a successful career at Roche, where he had been CEO of the company's Italian business, and his plan was to leverage his business communications tools, crafting a compelling pitch for sustainability in terms of profitability. Fitting right into the Lend Lease vernacular and building on his own background running a billion-dollar business, it was a message filled with facts and figures, charts and graphs. Indeed, it mirrored a thesis on the triple bottom line in practice that he had developed while at Roche.

It went over like a lead balloon.

"I was not getting the results I wanted. I was frustrated to deal with the same crap every day … It didn't fit well," he recalls. He was not connecting.

34

What to do? Pascal had his lightbulb moment after attending a series of conferences on sustainability.

At the conferences, he realized that there were two kinds of presenters. The first presented a basic, factual business case for sustainability. They were right, and they had plenty of evidence to support their rightness. But there was no passion in their presentation, no emotional tug that inspired. Then there were the others—the ones who framed the personal aspirations of the audience in terms of broader societal themes and wove their information into a more memorable and colorful fabric. They were making the same essential pitch for sustainability, yet they were doing it in a way that had a different and far more emotional impact. Pascal came to realize that there was another way—a better way—to go about the process of influencing others. He traded in his facts-and-figures-based tactics for a new influencing process: storytelling.

Pascal came to the process with some natural storytelling skills, but his goal was not just to weave a great tale himself but also to influence others to do the same. He needed to motivate this company to embrace storytelling as an influencing process.

In one memorable presentation, Pascal opened his remarks by standing before a large-screen projection of a black-and-white photograph of an armed man aiming his gun directly into the camera lens, as though taking aim at the audience. The barrel of the gun and the look of intensity on the face of the shooter were powerful and sent a shudder through the audience of one hundred managers. It seemed menacing.

Then Pascal began to tell the story.

This is a photograph of Károly Takács. You probably have never heard of him, but in Hungary many streets and places are named after him. Let me tell you his story. Takács was one of the world's most remarkable rapid-fire pistol sportsmen. In 1936, Takács was already a star in his discipline and favored to win gold in the Olympics that year. But world history would interfere with this athlete's plans. Political winds of the time denied him a spot on the Hungarian national team because he was not a commissioned officer.

Takács was undeterred, however, and he became a commissioned officer after the Olympics in hopes of representing his country four years hence. But the next eight years went differently than he expected. The Olympics in 1940 and 1944 were cancelled. Crushingly, his right hand was irreparably injured by a grenade. As the war ended, Takács had faded into the footnotes of Olympic history.

So when Takács arrived at the London summer games in 1948—now nearly forty—he seemed a scarred relic of the prewar era. And yet the man in this picture, Károly Takács, stunned the games by winning the gold medal, beating the reigning world champion and setting a new world record—with his left hand, on which he retrained himself to shoot. And he won gold again at the 1952 Summer Olympics in Helsinki.

At this point Pascal lowered his voice and stepped closer to the audience with a smile. He continued: "Look again at his

36

picture. Now what do you see? Notice how differently you feel, now that I've told you the story."

In telling the story, Pascal could feel the mood in the room change, from tense and worried to impressed and inspired. He had led them through the transformational experience of a great story, well told. Far too often, Pascal went on, we tell stories as a series of facts. He could have simply listed the facts in this case: Takács was a Hungarian pistol shooter. He switched his shooting hand after an accident and won two gold medals. Those are the facts; they can be shown on a flow chart with boxes and arrows, much as we tell the truly inspiring story of sustainability. But on that day, Pascal used words and pictures to turn a collection of facts into a powerful story, one that allowed the audience to experience an emotional trajectory—apprehension, realization, and finally, inspiration. Storytelling elevated the facts from basic information to compelling tale.

Then Pascal made his connection to sustainability and to the creation of a culture of purpose. Sustainability is perhaps the most engaging story we can tell, he implored his audience. Let's not reduce it to a series of numbers. Let's not insist on telling the story with facts and figures and PowerPoint decks. Let's narrate sustainability with stories. Let's use the stories to connect with others and make our case. And Lend Lease was working on so many inspirational projects that stories were not difficult to come by.

In this anecdote, we can see Pascal demonstrating his keen understanding of influencing and the way in which storytelling plays a role. By conveying the facts through a story, he modeled the methodology for reaching and influencing others. He demonstrated through his own actions—and allowed the audience to experience firsthand—the power that storytelling brings to the influencing process.

But, as Pascal himself commented, a leader "cannot be a bard that walks around telling stories" and hoping that will achieve influencing results. This is not an entertainment tactic. There must be a larger goal attached to the process. Storytelling is just one of the ways to practice the art and leverage the power of influencing.

Storytelling is often the mark of a wise individual who realizes he may need a little help to make his point. Effective leaders recognize when their own voice is not the most influential. Pascal noticed that pushback to his sustainability efforts often came not from philosophical objections but instead from habit. People can get into a rut of behaviors and reactions that block their ability to hear new and important information. Lend Lease was no exception. As in many firms, at Lend Lease there was an occasional reliance on siloed thinking when it came to sustainability. Each section of the company understood its own priorities and mandates and figured that what was going on elsewhere was not their department. It's not that architects and engineers thought sustainability was wrong; they simply had a way of doing business that they found difficult to integrate with these seemingly disconnected sustainability goals. What Pascal encountered, in other words, was immunity to change.[1]

To disrupt this siloed culture, Pascal began to bring in outside voices. He introduced sustainability experts to teams at early stages of a project—even at the first opening meetings—as collaborators. They joined early and became ingrained into the team and its mission. This proved to be a powerful influencing force. For example, having an ecologist or an expert in social housing or a guru on carbon at the table for these first meetings influences in a more subtle and holistic way. If the engineers are already considering capturing rainwater in an underground tank, the ecologist might then interject and suggest using a natural ditch to reduce the need for pipes, and perhaps then the landscaper at the table sees a way to create a playground within that design. By embedding sustainability experts in the team, Pascal allowed the practice of influencing to go on in a gradual and integrated fashion. Instead of parachuting in an outsider to demand sustainability changes at the end of a design process, he ensured that the ideas were incorporated into the design from its inception. The project was shaped at its core.

Despite its often pleasant presentation, influencing should not be perceived as meek or soft. It is a muscular competency that can be wielded with both a gentle and forceful hand. Encouraging disparate voices is a gentle form. Here's a good example of influencing that took the form not of a pleasant story but more of an order. Pascal was not afraid to use his implied authority as an influencing force. In his role as head of sustainability, Pascal had negotiated the right to sign off on every major investment decision. If he didn't sign, the project could not move forward. He decided, after quite some time of not using this hammer, to bring it down—not just to shape a project in particular but to cement his influence in general. Pascal began applying a sustainability litmus test to each project that came across his desk. And when one did not move the needle in any discernible way on sustainability, he vetoed it.

The response to this was predictable. His inbox, voice mail, and meeting calendar filled up with missives from angry managers, horrified to find their project denied. "They were outraged," says Pascal. "They couldn't understand that something with such clear money-making potential was not being endorsed by one of the senior managers. It created a fantastic moment of clash." Pascal had the backing of the company CEO, so he told the incredulous managers to go back and figure out ways to make their projects sustainable to earn Pascal's sign-off.

Although the standoff was dramatic and created tension in the company, ultimately it was a powerful driver of collaboration and of Pascal's ability to influence. Pascal's authority and his sustainability goals were made crystal clear. Managers began to design projects in order to meet Pascal's standard and, by embracing the themes themselves, over time made Pascal's standard the company's standard. Further, they began to reach out to Pascal's team early in the process to ensure their buy-in. Pascal, in short, used the inferred power of the veto to drive collaboration that originated from those he was seeking to influence. He knew that he could not keep vetoing, so developing that influence was key. As it turned out, a single veto was enough: as collaboration rose, the veto became superfluous. Pascal and his team were truly influencing the organization.

The impact was real and tangible. Two years later, Pascal noticed an email string in which an architect and an engineer at Lend Lease pressed a team of outside consultants to step up the sustainable aspects of a project in development. "I wrote to both those guys and said, the kinds of questions you are asking, the tone of your message, the way you are trying to get these outside suppliers to understand our mission and our values—this is great! I really congratulated them on it." Pascal had brought these leaders in as collaborators on the mission, and was now coaching them as they took up the mantle themselves.

The ability to collaborate with others across the organization is a critical component of this competency at its highest level. Influence alone can leave the audience without next steps. It's possible, for example, to deliver a highly influential message that motivates listeners but fails to provide them with the tools needed to achieve change. Collaboration, therefore, is part of the leader's mandate. Once the case has been made and others have been drawn in as teammates around a cause, it is collaboration that enables action and change. Leaders must pair their influencing efforts with the tools and processes necessary to turn the newly influenced into collaborators.

These new processes may take a variety of forms. At Lend Lease, new project forms were created so that even the most hardened construction manager would need to articulate exactly how a project would engage with its community. Sustainability audits became part of the regular process of recording and measuring projects in process. And Pascal successfully pushed to augment the company's bonus system to rate and reward leadership on quantifiable sustainability goals. By creating concrete processes, Pascal was able to follow his successful influencing with robust collaboration. The framework for the new behaviors came alongside the exhortation to embrace change.

Pascal's influence grew beyond the company's walls when Lend Lease built the Athlete's Village for the London Olympics. With a value exceeding $2 billion, the Athlete's Village housed fourteen thousand athletes and staff and was conceived from the beginning to convert into a new neighborhood—now London's East Village—for ten thousand people after the Olympics. The project boasts countless superlatives, from the largest land contamination cleanup project in the world to the first time that a U.K. mass development adhered to such elevated building codes. Perhaps most impressively, with 99 percent of its timber coming from certified responsibly sourced or recycled timber, the Athlete's Village became the largest development certified by the Forest Stewardship Council in history. Pascal is understandably proud of this massive project and quick to point out that it was made possible by the legions of others Lend Lease drew into the process, from NGOs such as the Global Forestry Network to companies such as Philips, and of course armies of contractors.

Pascal's experience at Lend Lease provides us with a robust example of influencing in action. We're able to see him develop and implement his initial influencing style and even "take it up a notch" by creating new ways to influence as his tenure at the firm progressed. Over time and with practice, Pascal became much more than a storytelling bard; he leveraged his competency in influencing to drive substantial and lasting change.

■ ■ ■

What we have learned about influencing is that, first, the competency requires the ability to modulate styles, as Pascal did in narrating the business logic of sustainability with emotionally compelling stories. Seeking and responding to the concerns of others, for example, he brought in outsiders to bust up siloed thinking that blocked systemic solutions. Second, Pascal fostered informal structures of influencing by making the most of the only time he vetoed a proposal. In fact, it was this incident that enabled him to package his implied influence in embedding sustainability across the organization's operations. Third, Pascal fostered collaboration—for example, in congratulating his architects for pushing outside consultants to do more and scaling influence beyond the organization itself. Pascal's work on the Athlete's Village for the London Olympics is an example of influence at scale.

At the core of this progression is the trust Pascal had to earn in order to influence others. Trust that he was not out to make life difficult for his colleagues but out to help make the company better. Trust that they were on the same team. And trust that, together, they would win.

Discovering the Leader: Markers for the Competency of Influencing

Influencing others is a crucial leadership competency, particularly during the early stages of building a culture of purpose. The reason is simple: people embrace a purpose not because it is mandated by management but because they are confronted with a narrative that resonates with their own values and aspirations. Influencing is the competency that leads to such resonance, and collaboration makes it actionable.

It's one thing to look at a star practitioner like Pascal in the field. But what about other leaders and those potentially ready to step into leadership roles? Part of your role as a leader is both to orchestrate moments that allow people throughout the organization to build this muscle, and to identify the ones most capable of doing so. They are the ones with the greatest impact on your culture, and you want them on your side. What follows are some questions to help reveal your influencers.

What to Look For	How to Look for It
These individuals use humor and celebration to build connections with others.	How have you used levity to diffuse difficult moments? How have you incented behaviors you were looking to promote?
They know the facts, but can inspire others by telling stories.	[Listen]
They enrich dialogues with outside voices.	When did you bring in an outsider to advance your agenda? How did you choose him or her?
They transport others out of their accustomed environment to inspire them.	When have you exposed others inside your organization to new environments? How did you select those environments? How do you know you have inspired others?
They use language that is accessible.	[Listen]

What to Look For	How to Look for It
They are unafraid of conflict; indeed, they consider it a useful catalyst.	When have you used conflict to achieve your aims? How did you go about orchestrating it? How, exactly, did you leverage the outcome of the conflict?
They trust others, and others trust them.	Who has been your guide? Whom would you nominate as a reference who would consider you theirs? Who else deserves credit for your proudest accomplishments? Whom are you most proud to have helped change their mind, and why?
They collaborate.	Tell me about a time that you helped somebody adopt a new course of action and joined him or her on that path.

Red Flags: People who are poor influencers not only actively resist collaborating with others but also tend to inhibit collaboration among others. They are likely to turn down requests for help. Often, but not always, they are ineffective communicators. In referencing them, you will find that people they have worked with do not put much stock in their credibility.

The Impact of Results
Delivery

In August 2010, a major section of the San José copper mine collapsed, trapping thirty-three miners 2,300 feet underground. Chile's president summoned André Sougarret and put him in charge of the rescue operation.

Realizing that nobody had ever drilled that far to rescue trapped miners, André effectively compartmentalized his mind. He could not afford to contemplate the full scale of what he was trying to achieve—and that it had never been done before.

For those trapped below, he focused on the singular task of getting to the men rather than consider their potential fate. He began by taking control of the site. He sent home some of the companies already working away at the surface, as well as the rescue teams that had amassed at the location. He would call them when there was somebody to rescue. Then he rode a truck into the mine to get a sense of what he was up against.

For those above ground, André's guiding principle was to resolve uncertainty. This was particularly difficult when for the first two weeks his efforts yielded no sign of life. He adopted a simple strategy: to prevent speculation, the information delivered was always true, referring to the facts and not interpretations. To this end, André chose simple language rather than the technical terminology of mining.

André assembled his staff, starting with his risk manager, who began by constructing a mosaic of maps to get a picture of what lay underground. With this picture in mind, his team began to develop options. As his team grew to three hundred, André stuck with this simple strategy: get to the miners; be candid with the families. Reflecting his unwavering focus on the result he was entrusted to deliver, he told me that "the rest we considered second order." No small feat, considering that "the rest" included politicians, mining officials, and of course swarms of international media reporters eager to assign blame.

On October 13, the miners were rescued. André allowed himself to contemplate the scale of what he had achieved, showing his own emotions for the first time when the twenty-eighth miner surfaced and was embraced by his crying mother and sister. As the remaining five miners surfaced, he says, "I could not hold back tears." By defining the right results, developing multiple paths to get there, and relegating everything else to the background, he had gotten the job done.

Results Delivery

What do James Bond and Darth Vader have in common? They get results. And those who consistently get results *like* getting results. It is that simple. Notice that Messrs. Bond and Vader are in the business of getting stuff done, not *deciding* what stuff gets done (they both have bosses). And although they may occasionally stray to further the plot, overall they are known for a constancy of focus that allows them to zero in on their objectives—sometimes to the detriment of everything else around them—and they can translate a vision into actionable steps that they then execute. When they are in action mode, you don't want to be the one standing in the way.

Results delivery is the motor on the journey toward a sustainable business. It is the engine of a culture of purpose. It is about being focused on getting stuff done, whether by iteration or step change. As individuals with clear abilities in this competency gain stature and visibility, the way they demonstrate their results delivery grows more sophisticated. The competency is supported by a personality of persistence and reflects the behaviors typically anchored in specific types of motivation. Key among these are the needs to achieve and to affiliate. People known for their ability to deliver results typically rank high on at least one of these dimensions and often both.

When we look for evidence of this competency, this is how we evaluate its power:

At base levels, this competency is reflected in an individual's ability to complete assigned tasks. The individual demonstrates desire to do the task adequately and expresses commitment to achievement by expressing frustration with others' inability to do the job or by being happy when a task is done.

At a midlevel demonstration of this competency, the individual is energized by a challenge or the opportunity to exceed a goal and sets new and stretch goals personally and for a team using relevant metrics. The individual may exploit opportunities to exceed goals, even under adverse circumstances.

At high levels of this competency, the individual substantially redesigns business practices to deliver breakthrough results. That may mean introducing substantial improvements to enhance performance throughout a large portion of a business unit, a complete functional area, or the company as a whole. This type of leader implements tested best-in-class or world-class standards. Results delivery may involve creating new solutions, business opportunities, or methods that can be measured by significant financial or process improvement impact to the business.

It is possible, however, to be a strong driver of results and never get above the middle range of this competency. This happens when a leader fails to consider the best way to get things done. High-level results delivery requires leaders to think about cost-benefit ratios and about taking more thoughtful approaches to improvement. The traditional concept of "results"—absent this more expansive outlook—falls short of what can be achieved by those with the highest levels of this competency. From a psychological perspective, this means that those with the competency to deliver results at the highest level are aware of and can modulate their selective attention.[1] They can take into account new and unrelated information, continuously validating (or evolving) both the desired result itself and the best means to reach it.

It's important to note that a strong competency in results delivery does not imply "a great people person." Indeed, it is possible to operate at a high level of results delivery and be a poor manager of people. (Darth Vader's troops never voted him Boss of the Year.) You can identify, introduce, and deliver a technical improvement, for example, with no human input necessary.

Still, although it is metrics driven, results delivery is not simply a "by the numbers" competency. Strong skills in this area often call for high levels of creativity and flexibility. Even the definition of "results" can evolve and change throughout a sustainability effort.

To illustrate this competency in play, I've chosen a company that is legendary for its adherence to metrics and results—the famously bottom-line-oriented Walmart.

How Andy Delivered for Walmart

There's a legend in retailing circles about Sam Walton, the founder of Walmart, and his famous appetite for rigorous metrics in his company. As the company grew, Walton wanted to end his television ads with this slogan: "Always the lowest price. Always." His advisers intervened, warning Walton that claiming to always be the lowest price at all times on all products was likely to be an unsustainable goal. A slogan like that would put the company at legal risk for false advertising, they warned.

Nonsense, Walton replied. The answer isn't to change the slogan; the answer is to meet the metric. Always.

In the end, Walmart's slogan appeared in a slightly altered way on the airwaves: "Always Low Prices. Always." The lawyers seemed to have won the battle, but Walton's devotion to meeting that metric remained.

Not surprisingly, if there's any organization with a fierce devotion to results, it's Walmart. Walmart is a company for which results have always been the driving force. Its approach to promoting sustainability and creating a culture of purpose was no different: rigorous and demanding metrics would lead the way.

That said, Andy Ruben, the company's very first chief of sustainability, knew from day one that successfully implementing sustainability practices was not a job for any run-of-the-mill metric. He certainly could not start with EBITDA.[2] To execute Walmart's sustainability transformation, he would run a highly creative and multi-iteration metric strategy designed to propel Walmart forward into new territory of sustainability, while at the same time keeping the company tied and powered by the skill set that had made Walmart a successful business entity. Andy knew that plenty of skeptics inside the company and cynics outside watched his every move on the journey toward greater sustainability.

Word of Walmart's journey spread quickly after a 2005 speech given by CEO Lee Scott, titled "Leadership for the 21st Century." In that speech, posted in full on Walmart's website, Scott explained how he came to see that environmental sustainability and business sustainability were not two separate topics but intertwined mandates that could not be ignored.[3]

Speaking about the environment, Scott recalled how his initial skepticism about what else Walmart could do was

uprooted by a lightbulb moment ("and that's a compact fluo-
rescent light bulb!") when he recognized the interconnectivity
of environmental loss and health. He said, "As one of the
largest companies in the world, with an expanding global
presence, environmental problems are our problems. The
supply of natural products (fish, food, water) can only be
sustained if the ecosystems that provide them are sustained
and protected. There are not two worlds out there, a Walmart
world and some other world."

Reflecting on how broadly environmental loss affected
every one of Walmart's stakeholders, from suppliers and
customers to associates and their children, Scott concluded
that "These challenges threaten all of us in the broader sense,
but they also represent threats to the continued success of our
business."

The speech was a great public moment, but the start of
Walmart's sustainability transformation had begun earlier,
far away from the podium, in Scott's office with his closest
associates. Scott wondered how a sustainability transformation
would play out. "How will we know if we are moving down
the field?" he asked.

Andy reflected and answered with a question of his own:
"Lee, do you know the Paint Can Story?"

Of course, Lee did—as did every Walmart associate. It
goes like this: Melissa Davies was a Walmart associate in
Bentonville. She was also a volunteer in her church. She came
to realize that the cans of Dutch Boy paint sold in Walmart
were presenting a problem for customers—a problem she
would often witness when she and other church volunteers

were involved in efforts that required a paint job. The big cans were difficult for volunteers to manage—especially, she noted, for the women. The cans also were not easily portable for small touch-up jobs. What did Davies do? She contacted Dutch Boy, explained to them that they had a packaging problem, that the paint cans were not woman-friendly. Eventually, she was able to convince them to come out with easily portable, twist-and-pour packaging that was more customer-centric.

Is the story true? Doesn't matter. It's a story every Walmart associate knows because the moral of the story is this: If you are a Walmart associate or a buyer, it's your job to do anything and everything to serve your customer. If that means going to a product manufacturer and telling them that their packaging needs work, then do it. Don't give up until you get what your customer needs.

In Lee Scott's office, Andy referenced the Paint Can Story and made this analogy to Walmart's sustainability efforts. In this first year, he said, we will measure our progress in stories: "We have zero stories that tell about our sustainability effort the way the Paint Can Story tells about our customer service efforts. That's today. In one year's time, I want ten stories—stories that will show how we are thinking about sustainability differently, stories that show our shareholders, customers, and society that we are better off and that this is a new way of seeing the world."

With that, Andy had his first set of results to deliver. He established the infrastructure to capture these stories, and he began with one of his own.

"One morning, I walked in the office and switched on my light, and I saw Lee Scott was sitting in my office. It's probably 6:45 in the morning. One of the things I always tried to do was get in before Lee, but here he was sitting in my office. And in front of him was this report with Seventh Generation that was just out."

Seventh Generation, the Vermont-based seller of health and beauty aids we'll visit in Chapter Six, was a leader in sustainability efforts and a longtime critic of Walmart. The report that day reiterated the criticisms. Andy had been working for months to arrange a meeting with Seventh Generation executives to build a business relationship between the two companies.

"So Lee is sitting in my office and the report's in front of him. I say, 'Good morning,' and he said, 'Have you seen this report?' Of course I had. And he said, 'So what you going to do about it?'" Andy told Lee of his plans for the upcoming meeting with the Seventh Generation CEO. And Lee left with these words: "I think that would be wise. The right question to ask is, can he help us to be better?"

For Andy, this was a powerful moment in his own sustainability transformation. "It was a moment where there was full permission for me to work with anybody and everybody who could make us better"—including Walmart critics.

This became one of the first stories in Andy's repertoire. Other stories came in from throughout the company.

- The Walmart buyer in charge of Kid Connection, Walmart's private label of toys, was among the earliest internal leaders identified by Walmart management to participate in sustainability meetings and brainstorming sessions. Inspired about sustainability, he went back to his job and noted that the toys were overpackaged. He envisioned a way to cut down on packaging and right-size the amount of cardboard used to wrap the product. The reconfigured box looked the same to the casual eye. It had a little plastic front, and the doll was still visible in the back. It was the same color and just a little bit shorter than the original. But it had been redesigned to fit a specific space—a step Walmart had never bothered to try before—and that reduced packaging saved thousands of trees and millions of dollars.

- Walmart's Sam's Club introduced a yoga outfit made of organic cotton. Customers loved it. It sold 190,000 units in ten weeks—and eliminated the use of two jumbo jet's worth of pesticides that would have been required to grow the equivalent amount of nonorganic cotton.

As the stories came in, Andy and his team did the work of making them into Walmart legends—just like the famous Paint Can Story.

"Our job was to use the stories to inspire more work outside this growing group of believers," he says. Of course, the stories were part of the quarterly "Milestone Meetings" Walmart held for its internal sustainability teams. But the storytelling did not stop there. Andy sought out the topics of supplier meetings and created content to dovetail with those presentations. His team created slides that told these stories, and distributed the slides to Walmart executives for use in their presentations. As the number of stories grew from three to twenty to fifty, his office created DVDs and sent them out.

"Every newsletter, every supplier communication—we basically looked for every available platform," he says. And from that launchpad, Andy's team then evaluated the feedback—which stories were getting picked up and retold? When? Why? How? Through that process, the same story-telling Pascal happened upon in Chapter Two became the very first Walmart sustainability metric.

"The objective was to get things going to produce real results for the business," says Andy. "Because for sustainability to be itself sustainable, inside Walmart, you need results. Lots of results all the time."

So by the time Lee Scott got up on stage in 2005 to deliver his call to action to Walmart's 1.6 million associates, he had plenty of stories to tell from within their culture. And he laid the foundation for a new set of ambitious sustainability goals: to be 100 percent supplied by renewable energy, to create zero waste, and to sell products that sustain the world's resources and environment.

The stories did their job, infiltrating the consciousness of the Walmart workplace, inspiring, engaging, and creating a new cultural imperative. On a metrics basis, Andy was far ahead of the results he committed to (ten stories that year). He knew, of course, that stories came about spontaneously at Walmart, and that progress, once focused on sustainability, would be aided by the culture itself. And progress, in turn—whether extraordinary or routine—can effectively reinforce desired behavior.[4] This was the moment for the concept to become more structured. Jib Ellison, the external adviser to the Walmart sustainability efforts, describes this part of the process as the methodology and mechanism element—critical for a company like Walmart to move forward. "When we built a structure," Jib says, "things started to really move."

Andy echoes this: "All the stories are coming up, and we've got all this material, and now I've got a lot of confidence to say I am doubling down. In January of 2006, we launched a network concept."

Walmart formally organized fourteen sustainable value networks, made up of hundreds of individuals from throughout the organization. They had objectives and goals—and a clear sense of internal competition. "We were always bringing the network leads together to share their progress, and it created a race to the top of sorts for networks to best their peers," Andy says. "We would do these sessions every month, where networks would come in and share. We would highlight the network that was doing the best and also the one struggling the most. It was all under the guise of trying to improve and helping each other, but I will tell you it was incredibly competitive in that room, and you did not want to be in last place." Suddenly, results were about being in the most effective networks, networks that exploited the stories Andy had collected.

Jib observed the impact that a results delivery approach had on the participants in the network structure. Numbers, he notes, were part of the inspirational process. "If you stop with some of the stickier, more systemic, almost philosophical questions, particularly with an execution-oriented culture like Walmart, you will get nowhere. People got excited when they could do the equations and it worked, and you could move them quickly up a curve."

Jib provides an important lens of the Walmart experience because he had an outsider's view of the experience. One element of success, he says, is the way the initial changes inspired Lee Scott and created support for Andy and his efforts throughout the company.

"As the process unfolded, Lee got more and more excited about it because he really saw it was white space. And it was not inconsistent with the business model. It was not inconsistent with their results delivery. It could be used as a lens to drive out waste, which was something, again, consistent with their business model and authentic to them, and it felt good," Jib says.

Indeed, that was surely a key reason Andy was picked for the role. He was an up-and-coming leader at Walmart, after all, someone who could embody both the existing values of the company and the change Lee hoped it would pursue. This was change Lee could embrace as positive, rather than as an attack on the way Walmart had evolved. "Andy Ruben was not an environmentalist, but a guy who got stuff done. They loved this idea," says Jib.

By the time year three of the transformation rolled around, Walmart was ready for more traditional results measurements. The company had a rich and growing repository of stories. Its networks were fully grown and routinely proliferating best practices. Now sustainability goals began to be expressed in hard, bottom-line terms. They also began to appear in performance reviews. "We didn't mandate separate sections of the review for sustainability at first, because it was not yet at a point of being able to measure it. But by year three we were show-ing a quarterly scorecard that tracked total energy savings, total waste savings from our storage and our logistics," says Andy. "We began to start tracking financial impact, even though we did not know how exactly to measure it initially."

Now metrics became personal. Andy began to take a wider look at Walmart's sustainability impact. "How do you keep the thing moving?" he wondered, mindful of the fact that Walmart had over a million employees. "So we launched Personal Sustainability Projects, and in six months we had 850,000 associates—store-level employees in the U.S.—changing something personal in their lives."

What can 850,000 individuals do to change the world? Here's one of Andy's favorite examples:

> There was an associate who sat in the break room looking at the lit-up vending machine. He thought: why would we pay for electricity to light the vending machine in the break room? So instead of replacing the incandescent bulb, he unscrewed it. He didn't ask anyone, just took off the cover, unscrewed the bulb.
>
> As time went on, visitors might say, "Hey, you need to get that light bulb fixed in the break room." But the store was proud of it, and they would say, "Oh no, it's all about saving customers money, and we don't know why customers would pay money to light up the vending machine in the break room of our store." So it became a point of pride.
>
> I didn't know about the story for weeks, and all of a sud-den every store is removing the light bulbs of the vending

machines in the break rooms. It saved $2.1 million a year in electricity, and we never asked anyone to do it!

What matters more than $2.1 million is the signal to the culture that these actions, individually and cumulatively, matter—that local results are the real power of sustainability. Pretty soon, no vending machine on Walmart property was off-limits.

"It got us in all kinds of hot water because what happened next is that people started to unscrew the light bulbs from the vending machine in the front of the stores. And then I got calls from the heads of vending at major soft drink makers asking what was going on."

The ripple effect was that makers started putting more thought into the ongoing cost of lighting their machines. It changed the way Walmart negotiated contracts, but it also changed adjacent industries.

And the ripples kept coming. Associates began walking during their lunches, for example, and as their health improved, they started picking up the litter in the store parking lots. Most important, however, Andy saw Walmart gaining visibility of hundreds of new leaders deep in the organization, all eager to step up and deliver their results.

■ ■ ■

Andy's experience demonstrates, first, the criticality of beating objectives and setting new ones. At Walmart that's table stakes, and Andy would not have become CSO had he not proven this skill. Second, once in the role, Andy had to quickly demonstrate new levels of performance measured by new kinds of goals—starting with stories, then networks that multiplied impact and made it personal, and finally financial metrics. Third, Andy redefined industry standards: getting the vending industry to evolve its machine design.

While the results change, the orientation that yields them does not. It simply moves on to bigger questions. What are limits to growth? How can the company be sure to keep pushing, as it did in deciding to extend health-care benefits to workers' same-sex partners in late 2013? Because when it does, the results can change entire industries.

Discovering the Leader: Markers for the Competency of Results Delivery

Getting stuff done—it's what leaders do. In the general management population, the results delivery competency occurs at a high level in 1 in 30 people. By the time you reach the C-level, it's 1 in 11, the highest incidence of any of the competencies in this book. And because those who can deliver results ensure concrete progress, they are people you want in positions of leadership in constructing a culture of purpose.

Results delivery may seem like a relatively easy competency to spot and foster. But you can't just rely on traditional metrics to measure results. As we learned in the Andy Ruben case study, some early results may be measured in things like stories. So finding the markers for great results delivery may require some creative thinking and questioning. The following questions will help you identify those most capable of delivering results.

What to Look For	How to Look for It
These individuals can point to concrete results they have directly achieved.	What's the coolest thing you've achieved in the past year? What's the next cool thing you are after? What are you doing about it right now?
Often (but not always) insecure overachievers, they have a need to achieve and affiliate.	What gets you pumped about achieving results? Who gave you the most meaningful praise? Are you energized by creating higher levels of performance and better ways of doing things?
They match the creativity to develop multiple paths to their objective with the flexibility to switch.	Have you created new solutions and business opportunities that can be measured by their impact on the group or organization? How did you do it?
They gauge the costs and benefits of multiple paths to their objective.	Tell me about a time you had to choose among multiple methodologies to get something done. How did you make your decision?
They insist on measuring progress and are able to break down the overall objective into milestone results and metrics.	Looking at your proudest accomplishments, did you have any indications along the way that you were on the right track? When have you decided to adopt an unconventional metric to measure your progress?
They exploit existing organizational preferences and structures in service to their aims.	Can you think of a time when you were able to take a shortcut by piggybacking on something the organization was doing anyway? Have you repurposed existing metrics for a new aim?

What to Look For	How to Look for It
They make results feel good.	How have you used incentives to drive your objectives?
	Have you ever reinforced others' sense of pride in results?

Red Flags: People with poor results delivery don't care about getting the job done or about doing it well. It's important to note, however, that some people with high results delivery purposely cut corners on occasion—let's call them shortcuts with integrity—if those "corners" are not critical to the overall result they are after. In referencing people with low results delivery, you are likely to hear others say that these individuals have resisted improvements, sometimes actively and frequently passively.

The Payoff of Commercial Drive

A funny thing happened when Edward Munch's *The Scream* was auctioned at Sotheby's New York in 2012. The price had escalated to $99 million at an unyielding pace, with infrequent pauses punctuating the staccato back-and-forth among bidders. With the number rising from the opening bid at $40 million, Sotheby's principal auctioneer, Tobias Meyer, managed to be both animated and calm as he whittled the field down to two bidders.

A member of Sotheby's staff, manning a phone to one of the bidders, tensely motioned for more time in a palpably taut moment, and Tobias quipped, "Do not worry. At $99 million I have all the time in the world." The tension in the room dissolved into momentary laughter, and seconds later came the bid of $100 million, to applause.

But Tobias did not miss a beat: "We have passed a major threshold—I think we can go on." When the next pause, at $105 million, stretched on for a moment too long, Tobias looked into the eyes of the lagging bidder and asked, "I have to ask you: Are you sure?" Another bid ensued. And so it was that twelve minutes after the bidding began, Tobias brought down the gavel at $120 million, well north of the prior record of $107 million. He immediately pointed out that this sale represented the new record for any work of art sold at auction, and later added that the painting "was worth every penny."[1]

Tobias was Sotheby's worldwide head of contemporary art. His trick? He calls it "smelling other people's desire. If you're sitting in a sale and you really want something, I'll feel it."[2] He views art not only as desirable in its own right but also as a solid asset class. And assets are bought and sold. Tobias was in the business of orchestrating the trade, often traveling to cities all around the world to visit buyers and sellers alike.

Art makes obvious the most fundamental truth about commercial drive: it is not about the cost—after all, a painting is generally a piece of cloth stretched over a wooden frame, with some colors added—but about the value. The value lies in what the art evokes in the viewer, what it means in the context of history—and the fact that nobody will drill in the Arctic and find more Edward Munch. The supply is finite.

Tobias's commercial drive stands out in the world of art, and when he announced that he was leaving Sotheby's to become an art dealer himself at the end of 2013, what he described was the appeal of the commercial opportunity: "A buyer might be in Dubai, or Moscow or Paris, and by taking advantage of technology, you can do business everywhere."[3]

Commercial Drive

Not long ago I was in London and noticed two faces on the £50 bill. One was John Watt, whose steam engine famously powered the Industrial Revolution. The other, Matthew Boulton, is less well known, but was the man who acquired a two-thirds ownership in Watt's patent and promptly lobbied Parliament to extend it for another seventeen years. During this period, the steam engine became commercially viable and commonplace, creating substantial wealth for the two owners of the Boulton & Watt Company. Commercial drive isn't just about personal gain; many times it has led to new solutions that have shaped history.

Like Boulton & Watt, all businesses, at least all good ones, make money. Even the ones that pursue purpose above profit know that whatever the purpose is, they will need to make money to keep gunning for it. Commercial drive is the oxygen of business: innocuous when plentiful and painful when in short supply. Indeed, many economists would say that profit is the yardstick of fitness. Sustainability, wrongly, has often been positioned as counter to commercial drive.

But the competency of commercial drive is uniquely valuable in a sustainability leader and distinguishes the very best ones from other leaders at similar levels of seniority. In fact, in our work with clients who have advanced on their sustainability journey, we have found it to be the single most important competency of outstanding leaders of sustainability initiatives and indeed of companies for which sustainability is a strategic imperative.

When an individual leader in a corporate setting can connect sustainability to commercial goals, the result can be game-changing innovation and progress both inside and outside the organization.

Commercial drive, in a culture of purpose, is about identifying and moving toward business opportunities that are themselves sustainable. It's about seizing chances to increase revenue and profit necessary to sustain the company. More than simply a change to good, sustainability itself becomes a major commercial driver when leadership includes this competency. Far beyond cost savings, sustainability is at its best in the creation and marketing of sustainable products and services, of solutions that have real and extractable value in the market.

At its base level, this competency is about being willing to work toward financial goals and having a basic understanding of key profit drivers for the business. A person in middle range of this competency is able to translate profit drivers into specific opportunities, taking into account external benchmarks and beginning to look ahead. At the highest levels, this is about generating new profit-making initiatives and applying this insight to fundamentally change the way business is done, profiting in entirely new ways that stay true to the DNA of the organization. In a culture of purpose, commercial drive is about mining the common ground between value and values.

How Curtis Made His Passion Pay Off for Bloomberg

The culture at Bloomberg L.P. is unambiguously commercial. It is a business selling data to make financial markets more efficient. The entity serves moneymakers of all stripes.

At its core, Bloomberg has always been a data and analytics company. It built an empire around the leasing of its Bloomberg Professional service, commonly known as "terminals." (These were hardware terminals before becoming software installed on the user's PC or mobile devices.) The Bloomberg customer base includes the world's central banks, investment institutions, commercial banks, government agencies, legal professionals, and news organizations in over 160 countries.

The Bloomberg data business has as its companion the Bloomberg news service, which delivers financial news gathered from bureaus in seventy-two countries, with thousands of news professionals averaging over two hundred news stories every hour. Also part of the Bloomberg media mix: the Bloomberg Television Network, a twenty-four-hour cable network; Bloomberg Radio; *BloombergBusinessweek* magazine; and Bloomberg.com, a financial news and information website. Every one of these—and every new product and service rolled out by Bloomberg—is designed to tie back to the "terminal" customer, making that hub of information ever more powerful and relevant. Bloomberg products function as a fundamental tool for financial professionals to reach their commercial aims. This was the goal of the business Michael Bloomberg founded, and it remains core to the firm's mission today.

But for all its focus on finance, Bloomberg—the man and the business—also has a sustainability side. In his memoir *Bloomberg by Bloomberg*, the founder showed that he had more on his mind than money, even as he created and built a vast moneymaking operation clearly in the service of other moneymakers. According to Bloomberg, "We want to be known as a company that not only takes care of our employees but is also generous to our community."[4]

These two themes—commercialism and community—were coursing through the company when Curtis Ravenel joined.

Having studied life-cycle analysis and full-cost accounting, Curtis had begun his career as a program associate at the National Recycling Coalition. It was during that time that Curtis began to think more deeply about the concept of environmental economics. "I got very interested in the idea that being an environmentalist need not hurt your economic opportunities." It was an idea that intrigued him, but didn't immediately lead him into a career mode. Indeed, although many professionals who gravitate toward cultures of purpose are maximizing intrinsic motivation rather than pay,[5] the notion that one must sacrifice one for the other is false. "I ended up at Bloomberg randomly, coming in as a financial analyst for internal operations. I ended up helping run our Capital Planning Group." Still, his interest in reconciling environmental issues with business was dormant rather than defeated. It would rise up again—in a way that he hardly expected.

Recognized as a smart manager on the rise, Curtis was invited to participate in a global manager-training program—a series of meetings and forums designed to hone the skills of up-and-coming professionals within the Bloomberg ranks. Curtis found himself at a three-day event with an assignment to complete.

"One night they said to us, 'We want you to come up with an idea for Bloomberg, and we want you to flesh it out a little bit. You have exactly eighteen hours to think this through.' So I went to sleep. And I shot out of bed at four o'clock in the morning. It sounds corny, but I saw all of it happening."

By "it" Curtis means BGreen—Bloomberg's internal sustainability plan.

"I worked at Bloomberg, I had a financial background, but I missed the environmental work I used to do," he says. With his idea, he saw an opportunity to help his employer achieve some environmental goals—reduce cost, reduce environmental impact—and at the same time grow the Bloomberg brand in a space that was already attracting attention. "All our customers were doing it," he says. "This was just another way to engage them." This was a new idea then, but a prescient one given that today, nearly all of Bloomberg's clients have engaged on sustainability.

Curtis's project was among those selected for piloting. But what was supposed to be a short project ended up initiating a career shift. After working with a dedicated group to design BGreen, Curtis first suggested a senior executive to run the program, which was initially scheduled to run for eighteen months. After some reflection, he summoned the guts to ask to lead the program himself. "I knew that if I played this right, this could be my way of merging a deeply personal passion with my professional aspirations."

Quickly, it became clear to Curtis that engaging Bloomberg in sustainability efforts would be more than just an eighteen-month project. "You have to have a full-time, permanent group that constantly pushes the envelope," he says. A temporary group of people creates only temporary buy-in from business units. If you're not a permanent part of their work flow, once you walk away, they go back to their old ways. With that realization, Curtis's temp assignment became permanent, and his group became a team.

Selecting the right team members was a crucial step. Three people joined the team from key departments in the company: purchasing, facilities, and management information systems. Bloomberg president Dan Doctoroff commented, "There is significant integration across multiple areas that needs to happen to do this the right way, so relationships are critical. All of the team members have worked at the company for some time, possess great institutional knowledge, and know how to get things done."[6]

Curtis's team set out to execute sustainability the Bloomberg way: with a healthy dose of commercial drive. As he sent his team out into the wider company to pitch the themes and secure support, Curtis drilled them on the importance of framing their sustainability work in commercial terms.

"We had a fifty-page PowerPoint deck with five-year projections," he says. "It was a pain in the ass, but we called it Shock-and-Awe; the team is all about shock and awe. We have to be more professional, more business minded, have our shit more together than any other group because there's so much inherent skepticism about what we do."

The original plan called for analyzing opportunities by evaluating projects for financial, environmental, and company culture impacts. There was a heavy focus on finding projects with strong financial savings as well as environmental benefits. Demand reduction and energy efficiency projects had the strongest returns. The savings accrued directly to the operating groups, which lent credibility to Curtis's team. But even though savings are good, Curtis had bigger game in his sights. The key, he realized, was keeping the action-oriented mind-set of the Bloomberg customer in mind. The customer pays for what's of value, and in paying establishes Bloomberg's own economics.

"For Bloomberg, it is about helping our customers make better decisions with quantitative information," he says. "We help them figure out what a company is worth to them." A significant portion of a company's value is rooted in intangibles, one of which is sustainability. Sustainability can be—indeed needs to be—quantified to demystify how it affects value. "We live in a world now where book value only tells a small part of the market cap story. So much is based on intangibles, and it is very difficult to measure those intangibles. Sustainability is one example of that. ESG[7] data is used to measure sustainability in the firm, and we believe it can make sustainability performance more quantitative, consumable, and actionable amongst our users group," he says.

Making that case for sustainability to his commercially oriented audience meant bridging a credibility gap—or, better yet, eliminating it. As Curtis made the rounds on this sustainability discussion, he brandished his pinstripe suit, his banker's haircut, and his focus on the Bloomberg bottom line. Over time, looking the part helped him maintain a connection to his audience while shifting the conversation. He moved beyond the initial goal of reducing the firm's footprint. Pursuing a more commercial mission, he realized, could expand the products Bloomberg delivers in the sustainability space. He began to reorient his work and reorient sustainability from a risk management tool to a product and services opportunity. "Risk bores people," Curtis says. "Products and services—what we do well, stuff that creates revenue opportunities—that's exciting."

Savings could be channeled into a new product idea. "We had started with the realization that we can save a lot of money. We gained a tremendous amount of efficiencies, work-flow efficiencies. If you have environmental impact, you probably have waste. You have waste, you certainly have inefficiencies. You have inefficiency, there are dollars to be had. Then we saw that it made good business sense, period, just to manage our operations in a more sustainable way. We then realized that there was a lot of information that was being gathered as part of that. And Bloomberg loves information!" Curtis says. "So we began to think about how that information could look to the investment community. We began to think about our products and services. How can you solve a broader societal problem and make money at the same time?"

That thinking led to the rise of new Bloomberg products under Curtis's watch. Let's look at three in particular.

First, there are Bloomberg ESG products, which enable all investors across a range of asset classes to understand the sustainability risks and opportunities associated with potential investments or counterparties as the market continues to embrace ESG factors. ESG metrics are used to evaluate elements outside the scope of traditional financial analysis—elements such as carbon exposure and human capital. Users are able to apply the data set to companies and review them through a sustainability lens. Bloomberg provides data on several hundred indicators for approximately ten thousand publicly listed companies globally, and is increasing coverage every year as information becomes more available. The ESG products follow the trajectory of Bloomberg's founding mission—to democratize information and provide transparency for financial decision makers. This service has grown by over 50 percent every year since 2009.

Bloomberg now also provides sustainability news, research, indices, funds, energy and emissions data, and legal and regulatory data, as well as screening, scoring, and other portfolio optimization tools. Launched in 2010, the program has grown to a multimillion-dollar business with seven thousand users. Essentially, this replicates the larger Bloomberg model, this time in a sustainability framework. The information becomes transparent, and that allows everybody to trade on it. This is how markets become more efficient and sustainability becomes a commercial imperative for all market participants.

Second, Curtis helped Bloomberg acquire New Energy Finance (NEF), now known as BNEF. This global business is a source of insight, data, and news on the transformation of the clean energy sector. The BNEF team analyzes and publishes intelligence on the clean energy markets—including wind, solar, bioenergy, geothermal, hydro and marine, gas, nuclear, carbon capture and storage, energy efficiency, digital energy, energy storage, advanced transportation, carbon markets, REC markets, power markets, and water. This acquisition reflected Curtis's sense that clean energy investments would continue to accelerate and attract increasingly broad types of investors. And indeed, in 2012 clean energy investment outpaced traditional investments for the first time.

Third, the company launched a sustainability website under the aegis of Bloomberg.com as a home for the many news stories at the intersection of business and sustainability. The site provides news and insights on such topics as competition for strategic resources and developing technologies in the sustainability space. The goal: a one-stop shop for sustainability-related information for any executive or policy decision maker seeking out information about the business of sustainability. To meet this goal, the product creators leverage the company's extensive proprietary content resources, and also partner with and market aggressively to the sustainability ecosystem of NGOs, policymakers, and sustainability executives at Fortune 1000+ companies. Although expectations were significant for this platform, traffic has been double the projections.

Curtis could see the impact of his efforts both internally and externally. Within Bloomberg, a stunning 87 percent of employees surveyed now consider sustainability a key part of the company culture. Staff have embraced sustainability in their everyday work experience. Pantries that stocked food for employees sported new sustainability targets, such as 25 percent organic and 25 percent locally sourced. There were reductions in the use of disposable bottles and cans. The Princeton, New Jersey, facility debuted an organic garden, and the produce went toward stocking the Bloomberg pantries.

Curtis concedes that he didn't anticipate just how much of a ripple effect his work for Bloomberg could have. "There are tons of opportunities for you to educate. The guy who is head of our facilities and supply chain used to drive a gigantic SUV. But he has four kids, so he started to think. Now he's got solar on his house and dumped his SUV. It's not trite by the time you consider our fifteen thousand people." And most of them make decisions based on net present value, which says something about the commercial impact of Curtis and his team.

Curtis's impact extends beyond his formal spheres of influence. HR and recruiting, for example, are not regular touchpoints for Curtis. Yet he is frequently reminded that his work has ripple effects in those departments.

"For the next generation of leaders, this stuff is highly important," he says. When new hires come through orientation, the sustainability presentation is part of their onboarding experience. "HR tells me that sustainability is constantly brought up when they are talking to talent." And these are the people who will be coming up through the ranks—the next generation of leaders ensuring Bloomberg's standing as an enormously profitable enterprise.

Curtis has also tracked the impact downstream to Bloomberg clients. One client, Osmosis Investment Management, sources raw environmental factor data from Bloomberg ESG. Gerrit Heyns, founding partner at Osmosis, explains, "We analyze absolute, observed data on energy, water, and waste to determine relative resource efficiency in a business. We have a simple investment philosophy. Businesses which transform resource inputs into revenue more efficiently create greater shareholder value."

The underlying logic is that management teams that have the discipline to minimize waste and maximize efficiency are also most likely to apply that rigor to every other part of running the business; resource efficiency can be a proxy for management behavior. The data provided by Bloomberg ESG help Osmosis measure the results of management action. Gerrit adds, "We are not concerned with intent, particularly with respect to sustainable, responsible, and accountable behavior. In our view, intent is only as good as the results it produces, and until then it is potentially pretense in disguise." For this reason, Gerrit does not speak to companies until after he invests in them: intent is secondary. To Osmosis, metrics that matter are things like the amount of water needed to create one unit of revenue compared to your competitors. Gerrit told me that the data Osmosis uses "is unpolluted. It's not adjusted for accounting purposes, it's not moving numbers into depreciation or amortization. It's a ton of smelly waste that sits outside the back of your factory. You can't adjust for that. It is what it is. So, it tells me a lot about management." He knows, for example, that BMW produces fifty grams of waste per vehicle that rolls off their latest line, compared to an industry average of about two hundred times as much. And having invested in the company and spoken with management, he knows that they have a plan to reduce this number further still. This is the kind of management behavior that Osmosis is keen to find and invest in. This investment strategy represents an innovative approach to value creation made actionable by the tools Curtis and his team deliver to the market.

Yet perhaps Curtis's greatest impact stems from his understanding of how commercial drive can accelerate sustainable business.

"My boss, our chairman Peter Grauer, used to say, 'Curtis, we are doing this because this is the right thing to do, and it makes great business sense.' And I would get frustrated and say, 'Please stop saying it that way! I want us to say this makes great business sense, and it is the right thing to do. If you say, "It makes great business sense," you got everybody. If you then say, "It is the right thing to do," you get "Oh, that's nice too." If you start with "It is the right thing to do," you have lost half your audience immediately because to people out there, that automatically means that it probably does not make good business sense, which is wrong, of course.'"

And the Bloomberg experience is proof of that. First, we saw Curtis identify and weigh different options for making money. He did that when he had eighteen hours to come up with an idea for Bloomberg, laying the foundation for sustainability as a commercial imperative. Second, he attacked both the revenues and profits by focusing on work-flow efficiencies (bottom-line impact) and products and services (top-line impact). It was this latter step that allowed Curtis to, third, conceive of fundamentally new ways his industry could help its clients create value (as Osmosis Capital demonstrates) and, in doing so, create value for itself.

Crucially, Curtis demonstrates two things: commercial success is not at odds with sustainability, and highly commercial performers will seek venues to unequivocally make that point.

Discovering the Leader: Markers for the Competency of Commercial Drive

Among all the competencies, commercial drive is rarest. Even at the C-level, more than 1 in 10 executives display low levels of this competency; in general management, it occurs at high levels in only 1 in 80 people. And because it stands out more than any other competency in building a culture of purpose, it deserves your full attention. Bloomberg's approach of giving its future talent eighteen hours to come up with an idea (in other words to self-identify) is an effective way to find those who strongly display this competency. The company's willingness to bet on such people—and, as with Curtis, make them senior leaders—reflects on its weight and import.

Players with a highly developed competency in commercial drive are not hard to spot. They're the ones who have collected awards for their highly successful product launches and their multimillion-dollar innovations. But who are the up-and-comers? Who is displaying the early signs of having the skills it takes to be a commercial driver? Finding those people is worth putting some time and effort into. They're going to make your organization more profitable one day. Following are some questions that will help you recognize the commercial drive of a potential leader.

What to Look For	How to Look for It
These individuals flexed their commercial muscle early.	Did you have a paper route as a kid? Did you mow neighborhood lawns or pay your own way through college?
They reject the notion of a trade-off between value and values.	What initiatives for the greater good have you been involved in? How could I measure their bottom-line impact? When have you found that the right thing to do was also the most difficult to pursue economically?
They can frame complex issues in the language of business.	[Listen]
They are unwaveringly focused on the market in general and the customer in particular.	What's the most important thing you have learned from the customer? What external sources have helped you generate new ideas for business?
They intuitively gravitate toward explaining the value of what they do rather than the cost.	Walk me through your proudest accomplishments and help me understand how they affected the economics of your company.

Red Flags: People lacking commercial drive frequently do not understand how their work contributes to commercial success, nor are they curious about this. They are content managing without regard for financial implications and are happy to work toward goals regardless of financial impact. In referencing them, you are likely to learn that they prefer the theoretical over the practical the more they have managed to progress in their careers.

The Scale of Strategic Orientation

The Iditarod sled dog race is one of the most challenging competitions of the modern era. To be victorious, you must finish the thousand-mile race with at least six of your dogs faster than over one thousand other dogs in the race. You'll face whiteout conditions and subzero temperatures along the frozen Bering Sea coast while taking care of a team of a dozen or more dogs, each consuming five thousand calories a day to pull you along. Outpacing the competition demands more than physical strength and mental toughness. You need a great strategy to win.

For Mitch Seavey, who in 2013 became the oldest person ever to win the Iditarod, strategy was key. Strategy, to Mitch, means planning winning breeding-and-training regimens years out. It means getting not only the dogs but also the musher into top shape. It means taking the right amount of equipment and supplies. And then there's race strategy.

Having paused at the final checkpoint while in the lead, for example, Mitch saw a younger competitor blow past, relegating

Mitch to second place. Still, he gave his dogs another three hours to rest and refuel before getting back on the trail and reclaiming the lead. In his words: "Every year that goes by, I realize that I have become a better musher because of what I have learned the year before. What I know is that I can't make speed without resting."

So although Mitch does some things very differently than his competitors (for example, he employs far shorter runs and rests), what really differentiates his strategy is that it is not reactive. "Many competitors race for position, but all I can do is to race my team as well as possible," he told me. "My strategy is not dependent on whether somebody else moves ahead of me." Mitch won the 2013 Iditarod thanks to his strategic orientation.

Strategic Orientation

Strategic orientation has been the stuff of legends. When Odysseus built his Trojan Horse and when King Arthur built the Round Table, they were thinking strategically about difficult problems. Whether victoriously ending the decade-long siege of Troy or fostering unity among barons to protect Britain, strategic orientation finds new and better paths to achieving aspirational goals.

In many ways, strategic orientation relies on the ability to manage time. As long as a sustainability transformation has not yet become embedded in the DNA of an organization, it is threatened by time. Personnel may change, leadership may shift, priorities may be reshuffled as new demands bombard the organization. Competitors may rally and multiply, and any one leader's hard work at sustainability may be overwhelmed by a world that won't stand still. Urgency may crop up and distract the players. Strategic orientation guards against these eventualities.

Any leader understands the meaning of strategic orientation, but not everybody appreciates its critical importance to the arc of sustainability and creation of a culture of purpose. Strategic orientation is the ability to think long term, integratively, and beyond one's own area. It takes an expansive view of stakeholders to your business, with a clear bias toward action. When I talk about strategic orientation as a leadership competency, I am referring to three critical and fundamentally integrated components:

- Business awareness: having a broad view of the market and environment and analyzing it for different possibilities
- Integration of information: making sense of things in a simple manner that explains complexity through a set of principles
- Action-oriented planning: coming up with a simple concept to explain how the organization needs to address a challenge, fleshed out in sufficient detail to yield actionable plans

When you look for the competency of strategic orientation in an individual leader, consider a variety of factors. An individual displaying this competency at its most basic level thinks in terms of present problems and issues. This individual can describe the main issues at stake in his or her own area. The person may be able to analyze data, draw basic conclusions, and participate in practical planning of work processes. But this is a base level of the competency, and sustainable leadership requires individuals who exhibit more developed skills. People in the middle range of this competency understand their own business within a group and industry context. The ability to think outside the four walls of the company is critical. This kind of person considers an alternative business scenario or option for the business, can develop plans for activities beyond the next twelve months, and adapts short-term plans as business priorities evolve for the company. When an individual leader moves from a low to a middle level of this competency, an important shift occurs: the dimension of action orientation comes into play. At a middle level, an individual displaying this competency articulates evolving priorities for the business within a three- to five-year horizon and incorporates an understanding of relevant markets, relevant industries, and issues elsewhere in the company. This leader proposes new ways of applying existing company strengths.

At the highest levels, strategic orientation becomes transformational, not just for a company but for an industry and beyond. Strategic orientation at this level goes beyond accepted thinking to create new business concepts that draw on and move beyond deep and complex insight. This leader synthesizes market and competition trends with other factors across multiple businesses and geographies to develop breakthrough strategies that have a significant impact on the whole organization. Counterintuitive, or simply new, these strategies transform the business in the long term. Finally, this kind of individual creates a strategy for a complex multibusiness corporation that accommodates conflicting business unit objectives. It is a competency that involves philosophy, action, and an ability to weave the two into long-lasting impact.

To explore the competency in action more deeply, let's look now at the work of Jochen Zeitz as CEO and chairman at PUMA.

How Jochen Led PUMA from Last to Lasting

If you stroll north across Manhattan's Union Square, you will come upon the Decker Building. This is where Andy Warhol's legendary Factory was based in the 1960s and 1970s, where Lou Reed and Mick Jagger hung out with Truman Capote and Grace Jones. The Factory manufactured art and lifestyles.

In 2006, the Decker Building became the latest Manhattan store of PUMA, itself a dominant lifestyle brand. Nobody was surprised to find PUMA in this trendy location. Seven-time Formula One world champion Michael Schumacher had all but lived on the winner's podium for the past decade, and Italy had just won the World Cup, each clad in PUMA. At the same time, DJs and hipsters had taken to PUMA, and while major competitors continued to bet on sports products as their main sales engine, PUMA had redefined its business to generate three-quarters of its revenues from lifestyle products. And along the way, the company had become a leader in sustainability.

But it had been a long road to get to this point.[1]

When Jochen became CEO of PUMA at age thirty, he took the helm of a company on the brink of bankruptcy. It was 1993, and in the three years since Jochen had joined the company to lead marketing for PUMA's shoes, he had seen as many CEOs come and go. He faced not only the internal challenges of a company that had lost its way but also the external ones symptomatic of a conservative business culture. Although in contrast to Mitch Seavey becoming the oldest person to win the Iditarod, Jochen was the youngest person in history to head a German public company, he similarly relied on a distinct and courageous strategy.

Coming in at a moment of crisis, Jochen took a long-term, strategic view of the challenges ahead with a five-year planning horizon. His vision? Transform PUMA into the most desirable lifestyle brand in the world of sports. No small task: a lifestyle brand captures the vibe of a culture, and that is difficult to do if your products are piled on discount tables. But Jochen had a strategy for revival that would get PUMA there. But first things first: PUMA needed a hands-on turnaround.

Reviving the Balance Sheet

Jochen had to stop the hemorrhaging of the business. PUMA had not turned a profit since the mid-1980s, and many viewed Jochen as its designated undertaker. Having initially studied medicine as the son of a doctor before switching to economics, Jochen now found himself the doctor of an ailing business that badly needed a cure—and fast.

He went at it with gusto, consolidating distribution to simplify the company's footprint and merging departments to accelerate decision making. Although many of these changes revealed strategic insight, others were more tactical given the need for speed. Predictably, Jochen faced backlash when he drastically restructured the company and had to reduce the ranks of employees in Germany. Most important, however, Jochen created profit centers throughout PUMA to drive accountability.

These measures cut deeply, and they resulted in PUMA's turning a profit less than a year into Jochen's tenure as CEO. And as soon as he had the breathing room, he initiated the second element of his strategy, which was the revival of the PUMA brand.

Reviving the Brand

Jochen stated in simple terms the opportunity he found: "PUMA had been a great brand in the past. It just had to be rejuvenated." Proving his indifference to the skepticism he himself faced about youth on the executive floor, in 1994 he recruited American hipster Tony Bertone, who was then twenty-two years old, to lead PUMA into the clubs and boutiques where trendsetters were hanging out. This hire was emblematic of Jochen's commitment to building a lifestyle brand, which required credible lifestyle ambassadors.

What Jochen wanted was results, not pedigree. Indeed, Tony, who did not go to college, rocketed from youth consultant to global director of brand management by the time he was twenty-five, ultimately becoming chief marketing officer. The kinds of things Tony did to win Jochen's trust were all about lifestyle. As an example, Tony dreamed up the concept of PUMA City, an award-winning modular space made of two dozen shipping containers, which, rather than being discarded, were repurposed to be set up at every stop of the around-the-world Volvo Ocean Race that PUMA sponsors.

Although Jochen was clearly willing to bring on additional talent in his area of expertise—marketing—he all the while was not only CEO but also CFO of PUMA, because he wanted to personally manage the conflict between reducing costs and growing PUMA. "When you drive a car, you need to control the gas pedal and the brakes at the same time," he explained. "I saw a disconnect between finance chiefs trying to hit the brakes, and the CEO who wanted to accelerate. I felt I needed to drive this car initially myself."[2]

PUMA's revival became supercharged five years into Jochen's tenure as CEO. He now had created enough financial strength to be bold, and began to partner with hip designers, such as Alexander McQueen and Philippe Starck. PUMA had not only reached the leading edge of its industry, but continuously defined that edge. This positioning allowed Jochen to return to the founding spirit of PUMA, which was anchored in the brand's affiliation with outlier athletic talent. Only now it was no longer Jesse Owens, Diego Maradona, and Pelé, but the likes of Serena Williams, Oscar De La Hoya, and Usain Bolt—all of whom PUMA signed not only because they were athletes on their way to greatness but also because they refused to bow to conformity along that way.

Jochen routinely ignored what market research told him (for example, that PUMA should not sell to women), and instead followed the strategy of building a lifestyle brand, wherever it might lead. "If you make decisions by listening to market research, you might as well pack your bags. Sometimes you have to be able to go with your instincts."

By 1999, PUMA's brand had grown so strong that Jochen took control of the point of purchase by trading distribution licenses for boutique stores. Next up was PUMA's proliferation into new sports. The company partnered with Porsche to design fireproof footwear and soon sponsored Michael Schumacher on Ferrari's F1 team. All the while, PUMA was becoming a more coveted brand worn in the clubs from Tokyo to New York.

This strategy of augmenting PUMA's sportswear with lifestyle leisurewear transformed PUMA from a discount brand to one of the top sports brands globally, and, not surprisingly, the price point of PUMA's shoes kept rising as a clear symptom of the effectiveness of the lifestyle strategy.

The company branched out into other sports that aligned with its lifestyle positioning and was soon found partnering with Ducati and sponsoring golf and open-water yachting.

And the world took notice. The *Financial Times*, which had greeted Jochen's appointment to CEO of PUMA with the headline "Just out of Kindergarten," manned up and designated him Strategist of the Year. Three times. In a row.

Making Sustainability Hip

As Jochen revived PUMA, sustainability became an increasingly vibrant part of the brand.

Whereas the culture he found when he arrived as CEO was one of survival, the one he built over time was one of purpose. Along the way, he increasingly focused the same unwavering strategic orientation that had revived the company on the next challenge: sustainability.

Just as PUMA City made use of discarded shipping containers and upcycled them to new life, many of the initiatives that revived PUMA's brand were steeped in sustainability.

Jochen had begun to think more actively about what PUMA's business would look like in the long term—indeed what business in general would look like in the twenty-first century. In 2000, when the company had returned to health, Jochen was for the first time able to hire an environmental specialist. "I was always a great lover of nature, but I didn't really see what we, as a business, could do about it, nor did I know that there was a negative effect of our business." At the time, he says, there was zero pressure—or indeed awareness—from the customer on this topic. Ironically, this afforded PUMA the opportunity to explore, ask the difficult questions, and develop a strategy to deal with these issues.

Jochen had over time become increasingly aware of sustainability simply by keeping up with the supply chain problems of a rapidly growing company and coming face-to-face with the proponents of fair trade in emerging markets. He realized that PUMA bore responsibility not only for what happens inside its own walls but also for what its suppliers do. He says, "As information about the costs of our raw materials on the environment became available, I realized that we can no longer just continue business as usual."

PUMA would have to do something different, and that's when Jochen started to gradually transform its supply chain, starting with auditing its suppliers annually and making the results available to the public. Over time, under the auspices of PUMAVision—the company's commitment to sustainability, creativity, and peace—Jochen started to integrate sustainability into the everyday thinking throughout the company. As an example, PUMA in 2009 opened the industry's first carbon-neutral headquarters, a sleek building powered by solar energy. Jochen says, "This was all nice and good, but we needed to start quantifying impact to manage it."

The question that quickly rose to the top of his mind, he says, was this: "If Earth were a business, what would it charge us to use its resources?" Business as it stood, he realized, was based on infinite resources and the hope that somebody might come up with something ingenious that solves the problem of diminishing resources. "Can we just wait for that?" he asks.

In 2011, after PUMA had begun to burst onto the sustainability scene with its Clever Little Bag, a game-changing packaging system that reflected the company's commitment to carbon neutrality, he made his boldest announcement yet.

PUMA's vision for sustainability had been so compelling that PPR, the company with whom Jochen negotiated the sale of PUMA in 2007, took it on board as part of their strategy for the entire group. With Jochen serving as PPR's chief sustainability officer and CEO of its Sport & Lifestyle division at the time, this development scaled his sustainability strategy across a range of other brands, from Gucci to Brioni.

PUMA and its parent company developed and launched the Environmental Profit & Loss Account (E P&L), which made PUMA the first company in history to assign economic value to its total environmental impact, from the acquisition of raw materials at the beginning of its supply chain to the point of purchase. As Jochen says, "Nobody had real answers, so we set out to define them ourselves with the E P&L."

It is noteworthy that PPR ultimately renamed itself "Kering" (phonetically pronounced "caring"), and its CEO François-Henri Pinault has said that the name expresses both the company's purpose and its corporate vision.[3] Pinault has stated the commitment that by 2016, all of Kering's brands will have implemented an E P&L analysis and that Kering will publish a Group E P&L, which Jochen championed both at PUMA and as Kering's CSO. "Sustainability is not about being green," Jochen reflects. "It's a way of doing business that changes the way we *do* business."

Jochen's trajectory at PUMA showed all the hallmarks of world-class strategic orientation. He redefined his industry and became a leader of it, not only at PUMA but at Kering, its parent. He also developed a new tool to measure the effectiveness of this strategy, the E P&L. Strategic orientation, at its highest levels, requires the ability to think beyond one's own immediate business, to seek and incorporate different and potentially conflicting views. Jochen has done that, most recently writing a book titled *The Manager and the Monk* together with Anselm Grün, a Benedictine monk. The strategic orientation competency also implies the capability to conceive of strategies that change the way business is done at the most fundamental level. An example of this is Jochen's partnership with Sir Richard Branson in founding the B Team, a nonprofit initiative assembling leaders—both corporate and nonprofit—to make business work better by putting social and environmental considerations alongside economic ones. What Jochen says he learned from sustainability is that "rather than have a hard shell around you, you have to start engaging honestly." And so he has.

■ ■ ■

Jochen's strategic orientation manifested itself, first, in the ability to evaluate the competitive context and develop responsive tactics. Second, Jochen translated facts into actionable insight as he made sustainability a component of PUMA's brand. And third, Jochen maximized his impact by integrating the complex and different businesses in the PPG Group with one coherent and synthesized strategy under the aegis of Kering.

Discovering the Leader: Markers for the Competency of Strategic Orientation

The military term VUCA, which stands for *volatility*, *uncertainty*, *complexity*, and *ambiguity*, has helped advance strategic thinking in dynamic and nonlinear settings,[4] much like the state of PUMA when Jochen first became CEO. Virtually all business in

93

the twenty-first century will require VUCA thinking, and your challenge as a leader is to surround yourself with others who can "look around corners"—no small task given that in the general management population, high levels of strategic orientation are rare (1 in 71), and low levels of strategic orientation are the most frequent (1 in 4). At the C-level, in contrast, we find high levels of this competency at a rate of 1 in 19. It clearly is a key differentiator in advancing as a leader.

How can you spot the skilled strategic thinkers? Look for the ones who are never satisfied in the present; they are always thinking about what the past taught us and what lessons the future is likely to hold. Look for the ones who are in the midst of a project before extrapolating how it will connect with or affect the work of someone else. These are the people who are thinking big even when they are doing something small. They are the planners who are looking ahead, trying to see around the corner, preparing systems now for the events of the future. The following is a list of questions that will help you determine who in your organization has the most developed expression of this competency.

What to Look For	How to Look for It
These individuals are change agents with a bias for action.	When have you tried to enhance an established process with a fundamentally new approach? What was the genesis of what you created, and what happened to it?
	How would you articulate the priorities that the twenty-first century will present to the organization? What actions would reflect these priorities?

What to Look For	How to Look for It
They naturally consider the long term.	When have your efforts been complicated by an insufficiently long-term focus?
	Who do you think is our most important competitor in the long term? What assumptions underpin your response?
They think at (and continuously synthesize information relevant to) the systems level.	What's an example of something you have worked on that started in one place before you elevated it to another? How did you go about it?
	When were you able to integrate different considerations in pursuit of a shared goal?
They grasp the components and can make sense of the business environment in which they operate.	What are the three key drivers in your business today?
	Which of them is most likely to change in the future, and why?
They will not allow themselves to become stuck without a voice, and look for venues that maximize their impact.	When have you felt that your impact was artificially constrained, and what did you do about it?
	When in your career did you have the greatest impact, and how did you get to that station?
They are deviously clever in leveraging the system to their advantage, not only ignoring but overturning the status quo.	When have you decided to bend the rules to go for an aspirational goal? How did you go about doing so?
	Have you ever repurposed an organizational process in service of such a goal?

Red Flags: People with low strategic orientation rarely think beyond the job at hand. They do not appreciate the relevance of strategic planning, and if required to forecast, will do so with a fairly static view derived from past conditions. In referencing them, you will struggle to find a situation in which they acted as an autonomous change agent.

PART 2

Hiring Talent with a Purpose at the Frontier

One of my partners is fond of saying, "You can train a turkey to climb a tree, but wouldn't you rather hire a squirrel?"

One way to separate the squirrels from the turkeys is to zero in on traits by asking people *why* they do things the way they do them, and keeping at it until you get to the root cause.

In the case of curiosity, for example, somebody might eventually throw up his hands and say, "I just *had* to know how it works and whether it could be improved," even if knowing is not strictly necessary to perform the job at hand.

Leaders must recognize and seek out specific traits in new hires, recruiting those who will help them build a culture of purpose. In the following chapters, I will detail the key innate traits of people who make up a culture of purpose. You can look for traits in everybody you hire; think of those traits as the scaffolding that will support the competencies that people will cultivate as they grow into leaders. In keeping with this approach, I will purposely focus my discussion on leaders whose careers were powered by their traits (and the quests they sparked) to show why it is critical to select for traits early on.

Although the selectiveness of your organization with respect to the traits of its people, in isolation, takes time to result in measurable change, this rigor becomes an increasingly momentous driver for regeneration and evolution once it firmly takes hold.

Spreading Faster with Engagement

Activist Jeremy Heimans can trace his taste for political engagement as far back as first grade. Growing up in Australia, when a debate over immigration dominated the political space, he reflected on the lives of his own parents—both of whom had immigrated to Sydney—and designed a leaflet, which he handed out at his school. "I felt responsible and completely at home taking action," he says.

As he grew up, his messages graduated from the simple to the complex, and by the time he was thirteen, Jeremy held his own against tenured politicians, who were flabbergasted to be arguing with a kid about issues like third-country debt and greenhouse gases. His job progression pinballed him from the UN ("The institutional aversion to risk just turned me off") via McKinsey ("I could not see myself helping an oil company extract more profits") to a doctoral program at Oxford ("I realized that I am an activist, not a reflectivist"), where he realized that no job would ever satisfy him unless it was in pursuit of engagement.

So he founded GetUp!, an Australian activist group that has engaged more members than all Australian political parties combined. Jeremy grew GetUp! by trying out different causes that aligned with his worldview and rapidly ramping up the organization on issues that engaged the public. It is no surprise that he found himself in the crosshairs of powerful forces. He recounts stressful times when he was the target of intense and spurious investigations, but also points to the fact that these efforts to thwart GetUp! only strengthened it as more members rushed to support the cause. Most important, however, he realized a simple truth: "I am drawn to the world of action. I intuited it as a child, and it's the right place for me."

Taking his skill set to the for-profit sector, Jeremy now runs Purpose, a consultancy with offices in New York, Rio de Janeiro, and London, which he cofounded as a home for social movements. In other words, Jeremy is in the business of engaging others on issues that matter—on *purpose*. Because he looks for the same engagement in others he works with, Jeremy's first question in an interview is "Tell me about the three most important issues in the world today."

Not surprisingly for a trait, Jeremy's engagement was never reserved only for issues of world peace. He was also an ardent fan of the Canterbury-Bankstown Bulldogs and would cry if the rugby team lost a game. Clearly, he does not only engage others. He can't help but be fully engaged himself.

Engagement

Traits are difficult to develop. They are literally about you. The good news in the case of engagement is that it can be tapped in a variety of ways. Some people have the ability to become engaged on lots of topics. But many of us who are not engaged are simply not doing the things that engage us personally and that in turn enable us to engage others. From churchgoers to soccer hooligans, people like being engaged. And as you will see in our case study, selling spirits may be interesting from a marketing perspective, but does not engage everybody. And when you are not engaged, it becomes enormously difficult to engage others. In a culture of purpose, authenticity is so critical that engaging others without first being engaged yourself is impossible.

Engagement, therefore, isn't just about being charismatic or having good interpersonal skills at a one-to-one level, although these help. We are talking about the extent to which the individual has the ability to think through how to motivate, connect with, and engage groups, whole companies, and, ultimately, the wider society. Engagement is a trait with many facets, and for individuals with greater strength in this area, that sphere of engagement widens and become more globally relevant. The individual is able to model the behavior and seek out others with similar strengths to populate the company going forward.

Individuals with this trait demonstrate empathy and channel emotions to inspire mutual commitment. They connect with others because they intuitively resonate with people's

101

motivations and priorities. Their enthusiasm, energy, and sense of purpose are infectious. By engaging the hearts and minds of those around them, they give rise to and help deliver shared objectives and mutual benefits.

When you evaluate an individual for this trait, look for insight into the impact he or she has on others; it should be based not only on logic but on emotional connection.

An individual missing this trait is not hard to spot. For the most part, the person does not disclose feelings or concerns and may ignore conflicts rather than seek solutions. He or she rarely recognizes the effort and accomplishment of others and does not demonstrate care or compassion. It is a common defensive stance that some adopt in the workplace as a means of self-preservation. But in fact, it's this lack of engagement that can create an unsupportive environment.

Engagement, when it begins to emerge, shows itself most clearly in the intensity of connecting with others. We are talking about people who are able to develop sustained commitment over time both by reaching out to others and resonating with the feelings of groups of people. They check for evidence of communicating a persuasive vision and develop others to continue to generate enthusiasm. Those who possess this trait are driven to do whatever it takes to connect with and influence others on issues that matter to them. They are the culture changers.

At a lower level, the individual is aware of the feelings of others, recognizes how others feel and whether that feeling is aligned with his or her own, and is aware of how his or her own emotions affect others. At a slightly higher level of the trait, the individual is even more responsive: responding to what others

102

are feeling above and beyond what they are saying, and adjusting his or her behaviors to elicit people's best efforts.

At higher levels still, the behaviors become more proactive, their impact more visible. Here you'll see the individual using both intellect and emotions to draw out others—and of course their authentic belief system, which is the way they themselves feel engaged. This person believes in others' potential to grow and acts to support their growth. He or she acknowledges the contributions of others and shows genuine appreciation. Engagement becomes action oriented as the individual reaches out to understand the impact that his or her behavior has on others, enjoys bringing people "on board" and sharing common cause, and reaches out to understand the issues that others face.

At the highest levels of the trait, the individual is able to leverage engagement beyond the impact of his or her personal circle, work team, or even employer. Here, engagement takes the shape of a force for wide-reaching and sustainable change. At this level, the individual is energized by engaging and investing in others. He or she can be freakily empathetic. He or she creates and communicates an emotionally persuasive story of the organization's past and future opportunities, transmits an optimistic but convincingly realistic view of events and situations, and consistently values the capabilities and contributions of others and shows how they matter to the greater organization. The individual connects through sharing his or her own enthusiasm and responding to the energy that others bring; is driven to connect and to create productive relationships with people throughout the organization; and is invested in, energized by, and committed to cultivating the growth of others.

This person keeps engaging with others (through feedback, partnering, check-in) over time and is driven to use whatever leadership style it takes to connect with them and bring them along. It's this highest expression that so often moves this trait from an individual talent into the culture of a company. People who are great engagers tend to be happy and positive, although that's a bit of a self-fulfilling prophesy, as it is this happiness that attracts and engages others.

Such a person is a bit like a virus: individually small, but an agent capable of hijacking the processes of its host to replicate itself throughout the entire organism. When most of us think of a virus, what comes to mind is an infection. But keep in mind that vaccinations, too, are viruses purposely injected into the body to strengthen it. In the case of engagement, similarly, the efficacy of the agent is no indication of the quality of his or her aims.

How does a personal trait like engagement jump from a spark residing in an individual to a driving force that inspires a company? To answer this question, I will examine the work of John Replogle, whose engaged leadership spotlights this crucial trajectory. John shows us how engagement starts as a personal trait that can be nurtured and expanded to function as an energy source for a team, a company, and a wider global community.

The Draw of John's Engagement

John Replogle's engagement emerged in the most personal of ways. Although it was certainly always something within his personality, he came face-to-face with its power one day as he sat behind the wheel of his family car, with his two girls

104

in the backseat. It's a story John tells as a way to explain the moment at which he understood that his life needed to move in a new, more sustainable direction.

> I was sitting in my driveway in the summer of 2002. I had been working on my mission statement, and I had spent a couple of hours working on it with my coach. Got off the phone with him, went out, and my wife had the kids in the car. At noon, she was off and I was on. I was going to take the kids and have a big day. My head was spinning with my mission statement and what I was trying to do. I got in the car. I started to reverse, looked in the rearview mirror, looked at these two young girls looking back at me, and that's what, to use Ray Anderson's term, was my "spear in the chest moment." I parked the car. I looked back at these kids, and I had the epiphany that I had been working on this mission statement all morning, and frankly that mission was all about me. I was thirty-five years old. I was president of a $900 million business. I lived in a wonderful house in Connecticut with my wife and two kids. I mean it was like the ideal world, and I realized that I was on the wrong course.

The moment in the driveway would tap into John's deep sense of engagement with his true stakeholders (starting with his daughters)—and inspire him to take that trait into his work and, from there, into the wider world.

The business he was running at the time was in the beverage alcohol sector. He'd first run the U.K. and now the U.S. business and had started to ask himself the question, "What next?" John had enjoyed success and personal growth as the company grew. But through a series of mergers, he found himself working for a leader he did not admire in a company he no longer felt strongly about. It became increasingly hard for John to lead his team with authentic energy and to inspire their personal growth. It was time, he decided, for a shift toward purpose, and six months later, he joined Unilever.

In this move, John models the first step in becoming engaged—selecting (indeed, insisting on) a direction that is personally meaningful. He realized he was not on the right course, but he clearly was in pursuit of his true north. For John, this personal responsibility for his own engagement is something he holds as a lifelong guiding principle. "I use a lot of techniques to pull myself up and make sure I am doing what I really intended to do."

The most vital of these tools, in John's case, is investing time in self-reflection, to craft and iterate his mission statement. This personal development allows him to align his goals with how he spends his time, and he goes through the process with a deliberate rhythm. Twice a year, he spends time reviewing his mission statement, quite often asking a mentor to act as sounding board. In January, he uses his mission to define his goals for the year; in July, during his summer vacation, he checks in on how he is doing against his goals. John describes the process as powerfully grounding and rejuvenating. In addition, he sets a series of priorities each month that will help him achieve his goals. On the flipside of engagement, he then shares these with his leadership team and asks them to do the same. In sharing, John has found a powerful form of commitment that leads to alignment: "With our priorities set, we are much more inclined to fulfill our goals, which, in and of itself, is self-reinforcing and creates great energy and a bond among our team."

At Unilever, John began to express his personal sense of engagement on a larger scale, one that sought not just his own fulfillment but that of those around him—his team, his colleagues, his company.

It wasn't easy, he says. Although his marching orders were clear—turn the business around—so were the constraints of the culture at the time. It was pretty risk averse, he notes. You were not rewarded for being an outlier. You were rewarded for delivering within the boundaries.

People, he found, were genuinely nice, but they would not always speak their mind: "They would kind of, non-agree and politely go about their business." John says, "I loved the people. They were really nice folks. They would be great neighbors, but back then they could be frustrating to deal with from a business perspective, just not wanting to take risks." Aware that Unilever's culture has since substantially evolved, as we will see in the chapter on resilience, John adds: "Keep in mind: my mandate at the time was to transform our division. I would have to challenge the status quo and work with others to make this change happen."

John was working with his team to break out of business as usual, innovate, and be nimble. He felt that it was his privilege to "to role-model this behavior to create the right energy and engagement." However, he first had to engage his more conservative peers on the leadership team.

At the same time, John was committed to his larger mission—one that now involved not just changing his own circumstances but engaging with a larger corporate audience to shape organizational culture into a force for organizational sustainability.

> I think the two go hand in glove. For me, the first thing that gets laid down in an organization is a collective set of values, and you have to define those very clearly. From those values, a culture will grow. I think it's really important to think about what are the things within the culture that you want to nurture that reinforce values and how you create reinforcing mechanism for those. So, what are you going to measure? What are you going to reward? How do you think about the processes that reinforce the right behavior? That comes down to rituals, that comes down to visible commitments, and it comes down to the process of recruitment. You've got to nurture a system. For me, once you establish what those values are, you think deeply about the culture that's going to support those values.

He set about creating the culture and the values in his own team.

Within this wonderful, nice, polite culture he found, he went in to build something new—something highly competitive, collaborative, and risk-taking. "We redecorated the office. We created war rooms. We had battle cries and slogans against Procter & Gamble. In fact, I had a board meeting once, and I decorated the boardroom at Unilever with camouflage netting. I made cups with battle cry slogans. I came in a general's uniform, and I declared war on Procter & Gamble." It was shocking, he recalls, but effective. "I took a risk, and I created a subculture at Unilever where risk-taking was encouraged, where engagement became the norm. And very quickly, we wound up having a team that was motivated by that." John here tapped into one of the most effective methods of changing behavior: the artful use of the unexpected. Fun and surprise, it turns out, are powerful drivers of engagement.[1]

John acknowledges that his success was made possible by a boss who envisioned change, had his back, cheer-led the team's success, and never wavered. It's fair to speculate that John's ability to engage won over his boss, too.

John was demonstrating one of the most important characteristics of people in a sustainable enterprise: the willingness to bring a high level of engagement to the table. A key metric of a sustainable organization is its ability to attract the best and brightest with its values. Those people will bring their passion and engagement, and they will refuse to live within the boundaries of what is "accepted." So they will cause some discomfort. But if the existing enterprise buys in to the same values these individuals hold dear, the discomfort will generally be fleeting. It is an important way that engagement can shake up an enterprise ready to move into a more sustainable phase but in need of a wake-up call—a rallying cry, if you will.

The combat elements of John's new culture were just the beginning. In everything he did, John sought to engage his team and the wider company in a more active expression of its values. At an executive retreat, for example, he made sure to hook up with the handful of "mavericks" in attendance to collaborate on coming up with a new internal slogan for winning.

"We called it GOBOGO: Get On Board Or Get Out."

The slogan itself rings with the passion of high-level engagement. What's more, in this story, we see an individual with a strong expression of this personal trait taking his impact to a higher level by connecting with and inspiring others with the same vision. It is a story about engagement expanding from a single individual into a cultural force. John was the vector: "We were talking about how we needed to be more maverick, and we needed to take more chances. That we were willing to push ourselves and be the leaders out there, and have the others follow us. And it was a really interesting dynamic we created within the culture and the leadership team. And I think as a result, I actually had some measurable impact in the years that followed."

John was always on the hunt for ways to heighten the level of engagement of his team and of the wider circle of executives at Unilever. This can be seen in the very early days of Unilever's now-famous campaign for Dove: the Campaign for Real Beauty, which we will visit in the chapter on resilience. That campaign highlights ways in which John helped tap engagement as a force for cultural change inside Unilever and, ultimately, with the wider consumer audience.

An early step in the Dove campaign connected to John's own moment of epiphany in the front seat of his family car. Team members were asked to videotape their own daughters talking about beauty. "They all see beauty in each other. They have real difficulty seeing it in themselves."

This was a moment in which an opportunity to promote real sustainable change—not just in a process or a product but in the daily lives of human beings—was emerging at Unilever. John felt it as it unfolded, and here was a wide-open door to translate it into action and help young women relate to themselves in healthier ways.

Fueled by this realization, the focus of the Campaign for Real Beauty took the shape of building self-esteem in young women. And it was on the back of that that the company launched the Dove Self-Esteem Fund in collaboration with the Girl Scouts and started to really nurture efforts to foster confidence among girls and women. "That, for me, that is the sustainability piece, that is the impact. And that has become something that I carried with me as a real fortunate piece of my thousand days at Unilever. I am most proud of it, but it is also the most lasting piece that Unilever gave me, which was this insight as a father of four girls—girls who set me on this journey of being engaged in the first place," says John.

Not surprisingly given the nature of engagement, this notion of pride and impact was felt widely by others. Both Patrick Cescau, the CEO of Unilever at the time, and Shelly Lazarus, chairman emeritus of Ogilvy & Mather, the firm that developed the ad campaign, told me that they viewed the Campaign for Real Beauty as a highlight of their careers.

One telling insight John shared with me is how engagement takes hold of an individual. When you experience it, it's an experience you want to repeat. One might even call it addictive.

111

"Once you do that once, you want to do it again and again and again. So I have been looking for all of those types of opportunities to enrich culture and collaboration. I do believe in transformational events that resonate with people's core purpose, and emotion is the best accelerant for business performance that you can find." This, of course, is the reason that cultures of purpose are so effective and so difficult to stop.

From Unilever, John moved to leadership roles at Burt's Bees and then Seventh Generation—all continuing his quest for engagement on a personal, organizational, and global level.

John recalls moments at Burt's Bees when he knew he'd broken through and begun to lead sustainability on more than just a project-specific level. The company is headquartered in Durham, North Carolina. The state is a wealthy one overall, but Durham itself has a poor population, with 20 percent living below the poverty line. Under John's leadership, the company moved its business from Research Triangle Park to downtown Durham in an effort to support and positively affect the community.

In a collaborative process engaging the entire company, Habitat for Humanity was chosen as the firm's partner. The project: to codesign a community with Habitat called Hope Crossing. Hope Crossing was a piece of land that Habitat bought and where the partnership committed to building thirty-four homes. Home number one went up. Home number two went up. The development began to take shape. John recalls a moment of engagement that coursed through everyone involved:

As the last home was being built, there was a large section of land set aside for a community park. We closed our office for the day and brought all five hundred employees together. In a day, we built this amazing community. Playground, park, walkway, pavilion, and a garden, an organic garden. And it was amazing to watch the transformation on people's faces. It was 102 degrees. So, arriving on a hot day in bright sunlight to build something, we achieved success, and members of the community came out to work with us—especially the kids. To paint with us, to build birdhouses. The energy was palpable, and I will tell you, there was not a single person who did not leave that day feeling like Burt's Bees was perhaps the greatest company on earth. That the work we did mattered. That the person on your left and right mattered and could make a difference, and you are so proud to be a part of that team, doing good in that community for so many people.

John has repeated this approach at Seventh Generation, where as CEO he championed a close partnership with a local school in one of the most diverse neighborhoods of Vermont. "While the school was a great beneficiary, I believe Seventh Generation benefited more," John notes. "We were able, through our time, talent, and treasures, to manifestly bring to life our mission, vision, and values."

These values, paired with John's ability to engage, allowed others on his teams to develop their own professional identity. An example of this is Kathleen O'Brien, who had been at Unilever for five years and was working in sales when John joined the company as general manager of her division. He quickly became a coach to her and others, and after he took on the CEO role at Burt's Bees, she joined him first there and later at Seventh Generation. John says that what he saw in her when they first worked together were her energy, drive, and tenacity—in short, her "edge." I had the opportunity to ask Kathleen the same question about John in a later conversation, and she responded that "what John does better than anybody is orchestrate 'Aha!' moments for those around him. He consistently puts people and team first, and he makes you dream big and go for it." What John sees in those he engages, in other words, is consistent with what they see him bringing out in themselves. Not surprisingly given her ascent from an internal sales role at Unilever to director of marketing for home care at Seventh Generation, Kathleen told me that "I would follow John anywhere!" And she is not alone.

John is mindful of the importance of drawing out people like Kathleen, and he has the experience to reflect on what is needed to keep them engaged. Too often, he says, companies lose sight. They lose sight of why people come to work every day. The purpose, the *why*. They are so focused on near-term goals. They are so dedicated to hitting this target, that goal, this month, correcting this number, solving that problem. It is the job of the leader, John says, to step out of those confines and to get up high enough to really see the landscape and continue to reconnect people in their everyday work to the longer-term vision—to give them the emotional reason why they should care. That is what engagement comes down to: how we go about building something that matters and that is built to last.

■ ■ ■

You cannot be engaging without being yourself engaged. It starts, first of all, with a personal openness to the fears and aspirations of others. For John, this was the "spear in the chest" moment of realizing that his mission had been all about him as he thought about his daughters and the lives ahead of them. Second, engagement means believing in the potential of others and enjoying bringing them on board both intellectually and emotionally. John does that by, among other ways, sharing his development aspirations with the team and asking them to share theirs in return. Storming into a camouflaged room in a general's uniform to rally such an aligned team only heightened their engagement. Third, we saw engagement fostered in telling an emotionally persuasive story of a shared future and making others shine in its pursuit. The example of Kathleen O'Brien, who followed John from Unilever to Burt's Bees and Seventh Generation, speaks to this dimension of engagement.

Understanding the Person: Markers for the Trait of Engagement

As a leader, you will want to ensure that engagement is a prevalent trait throughout your organization. It bodes well for your future leaders and their likely development into influential agents of change. And because greater engagers themselves seek to be engaged, having them around tells you much about your values and purpose. Much like canaries guarantee the air in the coal mine, people with high engagement will be the first to tell you if your cultural atmosphere is tilting away from purpose. They are your leading indicators of purpose today and will give rise to your leaders tomorrow.

These are people who look for meaning in their work and in all aspects of their lives. You see them examining, reviewing, and connecting with purpose. Engaged themselves, they are able to influence others, perhaps through charisma or persuasion; certainly by example. They are willing to put their efforts out there to help others become as engaged as they are with a particular cause or aspiration. They relish connecting with and sharing their passions with others. In making use of the following set of questions to detect the ability to engage on the part of people your organization is considering bringing on, keep in mind that unlike the competency of influencing we discussed in Chapter Two, engagement is a trait and therefore "always on."

What to Look For	How to Look for It
These individuals have the empathy to discern the needs of others and link them to their own.	Tell me about a time you saw and connected with the fears or aspirations of others to drive toward a larger objective. What, exactly, was the emotion you tapped into?
They have had impact beyond their formal circle of influence.	What achievement that affects others are you most proud of? Who helped you get it done, and why? When were you happiest building things with others? What people outside your organization have been most helpful to you, and how did they come to be your supporters? What will they say if we reference you?

What to Look For	How to Look for It
They are personally engaged.	Describe a "spear in the chest" moment that set you on a new course. What do you really care about? Would I sign on?
They regularly take their own pulse and that of others to ensure that they are on the right course.	What do you do to ensure that you don't drift off your chosen path over time? Do you have examples of helping others do the same?
They create customs, rallying cries, and rewards to engender desired behaviors.	Tell me about the kinds of rituals that have helped you and others stay the course over time. What did you contribute to those rituals, and how do you know they had impact? What feedback loops have you built to amplify commitment?
They are unafraid to rattle the bars (for example, showing up in a general's uniform to a meeting).	When did you decide to go against the prevailing wisdom in engaging others, and how did you do it? How did it feel to be in that moment?

Red Flags: People with low engagement respond defensively to feedback. Perhaps most obviously, they disclose neither feelings and vulnerabilities nor concerns and mistakes, ignoring conflicts and rarely recognizing the effort and accomplishment of others. They tend to be more prone to amygdala hijacks,[2] failing to maintain poise in stressful situations. In referencing them, you may also find that they have not demonstrated care or compassion. You are also likely to hear of dissonance between what they say and what others say they do.

117

Reaching Farther with Determination

When I ask Thomas Frieden, MD, why he does what he does, he pauses for a moment, genuinely surprised by the question. Then he responds with a question of his own: "It is Sutton's Law: 'Why did you rob banks?' 'That is where the money is.'" The money, for Tom, is helping save the most lives possible. And he is determined to earn it.

Since 2009, Tom has been the director of the U.S. Centers for Disease Control and Prevention (CDC). He found his calling in helping others when, on behalf of the CDC, he took on the tuberculosis epidemic in New York in the early 1990s.

The results of this initiative laid the foundation for a model of TB control. Tom then went to India for six years to help the government implement a revised national TB control program, which resulted in 1.4 million lives saved. But he admits that it was the hardest job of his career, a job without authority or resources, yet dealing with the largest TB problem in the world. "I would work around the clock, and I remember thinking to myself every night, 'A thousand people died in India today from tuberculosis, and what did I do about it?' Every day I would think that."

Before joining the CDC, he served as New York's health commissioner, pushing for higher tobacco tax rates, calorie content listings on restaurant menus, and, to the great delight of late-night comedians everywhere, a branded NYC condom.

Tom's determination is composed of tenacity fueled by an inspirational goal and the discipline to constantly question whether he's on the best path to get there, but underlying both of these is a fundamental commitment to matter in a specific way. Indeed, his response to my question, "What would you like your eulogy to be?" comes without hesitation: "A number. The number of lives saved because we leveraged information to help people."

Determination

As traits go, determination is about as subtle as a riptide. And about as indomitable. It will show itself throughout somebody's life and becomes more prominent if it rises to higher levels. Determined people succeed with long-term objectives in various areas of their lives.

Determination is partly about the willingness to take sensible risks. (Nobody can progress far without this.) It is also about the extent to which the individual can drive toward his or her goals in the face of setbacks, difficulty, or opposition. This is not just obstinacy; you are looking for people with the intelligence to find the most productive way and change course when required. Finally, you are also seeking to understand how individuals bounce back from setbacks. Some, such as those with an entrepreneurial spirit, may pick themselves up very quickly, find the experience interesting, and move on with gusto. Others may be crushed and need a period to recover. For a caricature of determination, think the Terminator: not subtle, but unrelenting.

An individual with this trait keeps driving to achieve goals of substantial scope and difficulty despite challenges. Those who manifest determination maintain and manage themselves to stay focused. When they resolve to do something, they will drive hard to achieve it, overcoming obstacles and risks with ingenuity and tenacity. However, they do not let strength of purpose descend into mere stubbornness. If they need to change direction, they will.

To mind come great entrepreneurs, who are typically highly determined to reach an overriding objective, but—less obviously—are also unsentimental quitters on any one particular path to get there. They can hedge their bets even as they place them and walk away before deciding to go all in. Once they do, get out of the way.

The trait itself has more than one dimension. Achievement-motivated determination commits to achieving a personally chosen goal. Influence-motivated determination commits to creating a chosen impact or influence on a person or organization. Affiliation-motivated determination commits loyalty to a person or group. Any of these dimensions may prove vital to a task or project at hand. In evaluating this trait, you'll look for evidence of commitment and self-regulation. An individual in whom determination is lacking is easily swayed or discouraged. He or she vacillates between ideas, defers to common wisdom, and shies away from taking calculated risks. These are red-flag behaviors in that they demonstrate an absence or constraint of this trait.

At emerging levels of determination, an individual will show the ability to work hard and accept goals, not just for personal gain but for the greater good. Significantly, the individual shows the ability to self-regulate—to remind himself or herself to keep at it. At a slightly higher point on the scale, an individual displaying evident determination commits to goals, maintains focus, and accepts taking a risk. The individual is willing to stick with a direction without getting "stuck" in a situation and identifies times when he or she is at risk for getting stuck or getting depressed.

At the higher end of the scale, you will see individuals who channel energy to move forward. They will find and use ways to redirect emotional drive and conscious values toward the fulfillment of goals. They like taking on challenging commitments, and they find new ways of getting the job done when unexpected issues arise. Individuals who embody this expression of determination are able to identify values to help channel emotional energies, identify tactics to reenergize themselves or to disengage from overcommitment, and set up an array of tools to help maintain focus over time.

121

Finally, at its highest level, determination manifests as a way not just to channel energies but to multiply and magnify them. Such individuals are energized by bold steps. They take confident and decisive action for the sake of an idea even in the face of personal or professional risk. They do not accept the limits that others assume exist; they battle conventional wisdom. These are individuals who do whatever the goal requires even if the methods are unconventional. An individual with extraordinary determination commits to whatever it takes to complete the change initiated, even though it may take three years instead of three months, and finds satisfaction rather than frustration in long-term, broad-impact projects. When progress slows, that person reviews the approach and reengages the organization to stay focused, instead of diluting the efforts with other activities or distractions. Individuals with extraordinary determination consciously align external reinforcers and internal values for an explicit purpose. They define how each piece comes together and are committed to drive tirelessly over time. They create an array of tactics to guide their actions over the full duration of a project, including external supports, such as social support, measures, and structures, and internal tactics, such as visualization and the management of their own emotions and those of others crucial to achieving shared objectives.

Our case study subject is one who presents a dramatic example of determination in his own actions. His story demonstrates how he transcended barriers to nurture this trait not just in himself but in the company he led.

The Muscle of Peter's Determination

For Peter Bakker, success is all about determination. When he speaks with students, whether in his organization or lecturing at universities, he has a ready answer to how he charted his career: "Ten percent brainpower—it helps if you are a bit smarter. Twenty-five percent is luck—you need to be in the right place at the right time. But at the end of the day, two-thirds is just sheer hard work and determination. Whether you want to build a career or be on the varsity team, you have to be really clear about your goal, and you have to be prepared to give it your all."

Peter's determination propelled him forward in his personal achievements and in his eventual role as a leader in sustainability circles.

Peter was working in mergers and acquisitions for Royal PTT Netherlands, the recently privatized Dutch postal company, when his work on the acquisition of TNT in 1996 brought him to the attention of higher-ups.

Six months later, the acquisition was complete, and Peter was the project leader. This turned out to be the platform for his career, as the business doubled overnight: "I was asked to become the finance director and then soon thereafter the CFO. I did that for five years and then I became the CEO." It was a progression that hardly surprised Peter. "When I joined the company, the guy who interviewed me said, 'Why do want to join this company?' I said, 'I am not sure I want to work here, but if I do, I am going to work as hard as I can to become the boss so that I can take it where I think it ought to go.'" But as he moved into the executive ranks and began to consider his own role as a leader, his determination took on additional meaning. "The word 'leader' in the English language—if you go back to its roots—means 'path finder,'" Peter reflects. "So somebody who finds a new path. You go out into uncharted territory."

It's in Peter's understanding of leadership that the connection between his determination and his ultimate path as a leader in sustainability emerges. For Peter, the sustainability call came to him as a bit of an epiphany, after he had been promoted to CEO of TNT. He was flying to Australia on a business trip—his first as CEO. He had brought along a file of work to attend to during the flight.

"I was traveling to Sydney alone and on that flight had lots of time to sit alone and think a bit about what the hell I was going to do in this world." It was a reasonable philosophical question, given the state of the world at the time. The twin towers had just collapsed during the 9/11 attacks on New York City. So had Enron and WorldCom in spectacular disclosures of criminality and greed. It was in this climate that Peter found himself in a business leadership role, and he wondered how the turbulence in the world should play out in his own little corner of the economy.

So Peter turned to his paperwork. "The first letter that I found in my mail was from the organizer of the Dutch Open, the professional golf tournament, which we had sponsored for years. The organizer congratulated me on the appointment and reminded me that the contract was up for renewal, so he hoped to see me shortly to talk about the commissions."

The second paper in his file was a magazine clip. It was a business article, and it explored the reasons why 9/11 happened. The story, an opinion piece, described the gulf between the world's haves and have-nots and suggested that the chasm had grown so wide that the have-nots have lost hope. "That's what breeds fanaticism. Then the opinion piece asked: what will you do about it?"

In the air with fifteen more hours to travel, Peter pondered this question: what was he prepared to do? Now that he was CEO, the determination that had always been a trait within him was seeking a new channel—one that would lead him into new leadership territory. The moment had come for its expression: "In my left hand I had a letter from the golf organizer asking €10 million yearly. In my right hand the very important question."

By the time he landed, this CEO of a logistics company had set his sights on a new objective: a new division of the organization called the Distribution of Health and Wealth Company. He cancelled the golf contract without asking any questions and set about recruiting other interested parties throughout TNT to get on board. Within a few months, his brainstorm at forty thousand feet evolved into a partnership with the World Food Program—a way to get food to hungry children in refugee camps.

Although Peter personally spearheaded the project, it's worthwhile to understand how TNT as a company was positioned to respond to his determination. If you hire people with passion and determination—people like Peter—you need to set up the infrastructure so that when they are ready to move on from their previous goal, they are likely to pick one that is aligned with your overall strategy. You would not want a guy like Peter, for example, to decide that he really wants TNT to be known as the protector of Turkmenian honey badgers. That wouldn't have played well with the organization's efforts. TNT is a logistics company, so a goal with a logistics element is fully aligned and organic to the overall infrastructure of the firm. Part of managing and nurturing determination is knowing when people are at the transition point and partnering with them, making sure they share a passion for your purpose—for example, improving the lives of people—so that whatever they lock in on is going to be aligned.

Even with alignment, it wasn't all smooth sailing. The first executive Peter tapped to lead the project internally complained that he thought Peter was demoting him by handing him a charity project. Externally, Peter faced criticism from other business leaders.

> I announced the partnership with the World Food Program in December 2002, and we had taken a year to come up with the ideas to make an agreement with them. So in January 2003, I was at the New Year's reception of the Dutch queen, as always waiting in a long queue. A guy comes up to me, a CEO of another large Dutch company, about a generation older than I am. He looks around and said, "I'm probably your only friend in the queue. Can I give you some friendly advice?" I said, "Yes, advice from a friend is always good." He said, "I have been a CEO for a while. I know you are

126

new in the job, and you are very young. I'm really glad for you, but if I were you, I would just focus on making profit and stop this nonsense of feeding hungry children. You know that is for the government, not for business. You're going to pay a price if you don't stop it." So I said, "Thanks for the advice."

Which Peter promptly ignored.

Peter met that same "adviser" every year in the line, waiting for his turn in front of the queen, always receiving variations of the same advice.

But that was hardly Peter's only dealing with naysayers. At times, Peter's own bosses were concerned about the direction in which Peter was leading. Peter was not shy about making his commitment to sustainability part of his message to shareholders. But Peter's superiors were not always supportive of his outside-the-box behavior. A good example of determination at work, Peter was more likely to take initiative and forge ahead with a plan rather than ask permission.

I figured it's my choice; I don't need to go to my board to make such a decision. They are not appointing me as CEO to ask that kind of stuff. So I just did it. But then, in the first shareholder meeting, where I presented the CEO report, I had included one slide which was showing a Formula One car and another slide showing food distribution somewhere in Afghanistan. I said, "This is not a formal vote, but if you shareholders had to advise me—should I put our TNT sticker on the Formula One car or on the project that is about helping the world?" Of course the majority of hands went up for the food distribution.

Predictably, Peter's chairman confronted him afterward because Peter had not told him about these slides. "He said, 'I do not want you to ever do that again. You surprised me, and I would not have approved if you had asked me this.' I said, 'I am sorry.'" Peter chuckles. "My mistake, but I got away with it."

But even as he smoothed things over with his boss, Peter remained committed to his goal—and his tactics. He drew strength from the positive response of the shareholders, and indeed, a later meeting showed that he was hitting a chord with them in his sustainability messaging.

Every shareholder meeting, we would have three minutes of me updating them on whatever we were doing on the World Food Program and climate change. But one year, our logistics business was really under a lot of financial stress. My chairman came up to me and said, "I want you to talk about the difficulties in logistics and our strategic options only. I do not want you to present anything to do with your hungry children to our shareholders today. I want you to focus on the business you run and the things you are thinking about doing there. Is that agreed?" So I behaved this time, even though I thought it unwise. After my presentation, I sat down again, and then all of a sudden a shareholder stands up, and he said, "Mr. Bakker, thank you for your remarks, and we are very glad that you are so focused on the business, but where is your update on the things you are doing around the World

Food Program?" So I said, "Well, why don't we ask the chairman to take that question. I'm really focused on logistics, as you can understand." So then, five minutes later, another shareholder stood up and asked whether we had ever considered splitting the dividend payout with the World Food Program.

Peter laughed at the memory: "I thought my chairman was having a heart attack."

That might have been the apex of Peter's efforts, until one day, when telling his story on a panel to discuss sustainability, he was challenged to take his efforts even one step further. Peter was last to speak on the dais and only had a few minutes, as his illustrious predecessors had run over their allotted time, so he spoke about what had happened to him days before. He'd made a visit to Africa—an eight-hour flight from his headquarters, and another hour drive by jeep. And there, he came face-to-face with a young girl in a hut, crying next to her ailing mother because she would soon be an orphan. Peter recounted for the audience the power of this experience—to be mere hours from his comfortable first-world life and feel the reality of poverty. Then the lights came up, and Peter looked out into the audience. There he saw actress Angelina Jolie in tears. Just as he was allowing himself to feel proud of his performance, this happened:

> I got some compliments for my words and then a guy comes running up to me and says, "Peter, great speech. But you're aiming at the wrong goal." I said, "What do you mean, I'm aiming at the wrong goal? What can possibly be wrong about eradicating child hunger?" He said, "No, no, that is

OK, but you should focus on climate change because if you don't, thirst or drowning are going to be bigger problems than hunger is today." I was really well under way thinking about what can companies do beyond making money, and I had never thought about climate change, up until that moment.

Peter left the meeting room and called his office to give them a new directive: What are we doing about climate change? And this would take him into the heart of the debate around business and sustainability. It was one thing to get food to hungry children. It was quite another—for a logistics company—to start talking about what transportation does to the planet.

"It is directly related to the core business of a transport company. Basically all a transport company does is emit CO_2, and so when you are getting serious about making your core business sustainable, that leads to a whole new way of thinking. If we want to get to a leading position in fighting climate change as a transport company, we have to completely redesign how we measure ourselves and our performance in this light."

If you want to reduce CO_2 in a transport business, you need to get inside the heads of fifty thousand drivers and understand their work and their tolerance for change. You need to think about the equipment to use. You need to think about how you measure the CO_2. You need to help customers think about whether they really need that product from China shipped overnight. It was a moment when Peter began to integrate sustainability into the performance of the business.

Perhaps less sexy than the food program that made a film star tear up, but far more important to TNT's purpose.

It took patience and years of hard work to change this global transport business. But as the transformation took hold, Peter was determined to see TNT recognized on the global stage. He petitioned for admission to the Dow Jones Sustainability Index—a benchmark of sustainable companies. In the first year, TNT was turned down. But in the second year, it was selected. The following year, another level of honor was awarded to TNT: Supersector Leader.

It is worth reiterating that determination comes at a cost, as we saw in Tom Frieden's daily auto-catechism early in this chapter. As a trait, determination is not always easy on an individual's personal relationships. Peter has long recognized the impact of his personal determination on his private life, allowing that determination can sometimes crowd out the ability to maintain relationships. He acknowledges that the same single-minded focus and determination that drove his ascent to become CEO before turning forty contributed to the breakup of his first marriage. His signature trait was apparent early on—for example, when, having foregone dances with girls to rest up for competition, he earned his spot on the hockey A-team for eighteen-year-olds when he was just fifteen. Indeed, the "Marshmallow Test" famously showed that even at the age of four, the ability of children to delay gratification is not only discernible but predictive decades into the future.[1] Highly determined people, not surprisingly, are marshmallow resistant. And sometimes that means missing out.

Ultimately, the energy and restlessness that propelled Peter through TNT's ranks locked in on new goals. "When you're given the opportunity to be in a leading position, you should never overstay your welcome," he says. And shortly after leaving TNT in 2011, he took the role of the president of the World Business Council for Sustainable Development—a CEO-led, global association of two hundred companies dealing with business and sustainability. When we met for dinner in New York, he shared that as he was coming across the bridge from JFK airport, he remembered that when he worked for TNT, he always was in town to meet shareholders. This time, determined to face the next great challenge ahead, he says, "It is only to help save the world."

■ ■ ■

Determination, first of all, means committing to a direction and accepting the costs and risks implicit in its pursuit. Peter has done this throughout his life, from hockey playing as a teenager to his corporate career. Second, determined people are attracted to and energized by challenging commitments. They learn from failure—indeed, they tellingly reframe what could be moments of failure as catalysts of growth. Peter's definition of a leader as a pathfinder, as well as his vision to shift TNT's brand from F1 racing to third-world food aid, despite a run-in with his chairman that would have scarred many CEOs, are examples of this. Third, determination means confidence and decisiveness to go for it regardless of personal risks, as Peter showed in ignoring the advice about "how things work" from a captain of industry at the queen's reception. Critically, determination means not getting stuck. When Peter switched from child hunger to climate change, he demonstrated this nimbleness, which is not adverse but reinforcing to determination.

Understanding the Person: Markers for the Trait of Determination

Determined people are easy to spot but not easy to manage. Make no mistake about it: people with determination can be a handful. But if you want to be certain that, throughout your organization, people are getting stuff done, determined people are your strongest allies. Because they can break quite a few eggs (but make a great omelet), the challenge is less in identifying them than in ensuring that what they have locked in on is aligned with your strategy. And this is where a culture of purpose shines: the people you bring on board will increasingly be there because of your purpose. And if they are determined, they will add a ton of firepower.

The important guideline for a leader is to seek true determination—and not its brute cousin, stubbornness. You are not looking for people who pick a path and then mulishly dig in their heels. Determination is not about shrugging off all advice or orders. Determination is an inner force that keeps an individual moving forward against all obstacles and challenges. The following questions will help those in your organization who are tasked with hiring people ascertain the trait of determination.

What to Look For	How to Look for It
These individuals refuse to accept generally acknowledged constraints.	What do you do when unexpected issues arise? Have you found new ways of doing things? What conventional wisdom is most idiotic in our industry?
They are conscious of and believe in the power of determination.	What are you most proud to have achieved? What role, specifically, did determination play in this achievement? Whom do you admire for their achievements? Why?
They systematically create moments of opportunity and are ready to seize them.	Tell me about a cause you have been invested in for a while. What have you done about it? When have you achieved substantial goals despite challenges? What was the tipping point, and how did it come about?
They are unafraid both to publically state their goals and to take action without asking.	When have you gone out on a limb with a goal you alone thought was possible? Have you ever gotten in trouble for charging ahead? What was the situation and your task; what did you do?
They are dissatisfied with what's in the bag and crave a new goal as soon as their last one has been achieved.	You shared a major achievement—thank you. How did it feel to have done it at that moment and in the days and weeks that followed? What's next?
They are capable of "trading up" in favor of bigger goals.	Have you changed your mind on a long-term objective? What precipitated that moment, and what did you do about it?

Red Flags: People with low determination are easily swayed or discouraged from novel approaches and as a result tend to vacillate between ideas. They have a preference of deferring to common wisdom and tend to shy away from taking calculated risks. In referencing them, you are likely to hear that they were reluctant or unable to articulate goals or priorities beyond those imposed by others in their areas of responsibility.

Going Deeper
with Insight

In the spring of 1983, driving along a road in northern California, Kary Mullis conceived of a process we now know as polymerase chain reaction (PCR). PCR is a method of generating millions of copies of a particular DNA sequence from a single precursor. Its discovery has made possible a wide range of applications, from the genetic fingerprinting you've seen tie suspected criminals to the scene of the crime (or exonerate the falsely convicted years later) to the early diagnosis of leukemia.

Yet what makes PCR a great example of insight isn't just that it happened to turn out to be a big deal. It isn't that it earned Kary the Nobel Prize a decade later. It is that, unlike others who had come close to the concept of PCR, Kary stood alone in foreseeing its power to change the world. Kary, a PhD biochemist and accomplished surfer who ran a bakery along the way, knew that PCR heralded a new age in biochemistry. He was so sure, he pulled over on Route 128 where it meets Pomo Tierra Ranch Road and recorded the mile marker (46.58) so that history could take note of the spot. At that moment, genetics as we know it began.

When I asked him what fuels moments of insight, Kary responded, "Paying attention, being curious about everything, understanding your assumptions, questioning authority—and figuring it out for yourself."

Insight

Insight need not be the singular, momentous epiphany warranting a full-throated "Eureka!" (Good thing, too, since running home naked like Archimedes could backfire in the age of Instagram.) In fact, insight can arise more gradually, and usually does. Great insight is not just a moment of discovery; it can be the driver of a career's worth of success and impact. Whether insight takes an instant or a decade is immaterial. What's important is the clarity of the idea as it takes shape.

Lack of insight is often the unacknowledged barrier to success. You probably know academically bright people who don't seem to manage to exploit their intelligence effectively. They should be doing better, but they're not. They may not know why themselves. And this can be a function of poor insight. Insight goes beyond IQ and into *how* people think. Can they think big picture and also drill into the detail? Are they sufficiently analytical, or do they start from a conviction of having the answer? Are they also creative and conceptual? And can they translate and recycle disparate experiences?

Those who can are not just smart; they are insightful.

Insight is a trait—a thread within an individual that runs through every aspect of the person's life. But although it is often highly personal, it is also a tool that can be used in the service of a group, a team, an organization, or a community. When it comes to leading sustainable change, insight is critical. It is the lens that allows people to picture the extraordinary.

An individual displaying insight makes sense of complex information, discovering new relationships that, when applied, transform existing views or set new directions. This person can process a vast range of data from many kinds of sources and use it to shape the insights that make sense of the big picture and set a clear path for transformative action. This is where conceptualization, creativity, and energy meet. As a trait, insight can be discerned early in life, and in a noteworthy parallel to educational psychology, Bloom's Taxonomy maps the transition from lower-order learning objectives like remembering and understanding to higher-order ones like evaluating and creating. Insight thrives among the latter, and you can find evidence for it even in childhood.

When insight is absent or constrained, you will see an individual who thinks through issues from a narrow perspective, gets stuck in accustomed thinking patterns, and relies on past assumptions. This is someone who rarely asks "what if" questions and, when facing complex data, tends to fall back on what he or she already knows rather than grappling with the unknown or ambiguous. This contrasts with even the most basic display of insight, in which an individual is able to embrace different views.

In 2007, world-famous violinist Joshua Bell performed as a street musician in a Washington metro station. He played an instrument worth $3.5 million; his concert that evening was sold out at $100 per seat; yet he made only $32 as a street performer, as scarcely anybody took note. The same phenomenon we came across in Chapter Three, *selective attention*, is at work here: it's easy to miss what you aren't looking for. An individual with a medium level of insight, by contrast, will be open to the full spectrum of possible information. At this level, individuals are able to begin leveraging the trait not just for personal advancement but also for the good of the larger group, such as a work team. He or she can start with a strategic problem and probe down to detail, reverse course with nuanced questions, and link up to larger issues. The individual can shift through a spectrum of concepts and back again, recognizing patterns in complex information and uncovering new organizational issues to solve or opportunities to leverage.

At its highest level, insight is used not just to make a positive impact on one person or even an organization, but also for the greater good. An individual at this level is energized by creating transformational insights. He or she connects seemingly unrelated questions, problems, or ideas from different fields. This ability is often referred to as *fluid intelligence*, and it allows those who possess it to deliberately assemble new perspectives or realign those of the organization.[1] He or she is energized by asking "what if" and "why not" questions. How will this affect the business, industry, or market? This individual detects small details in the behaviors and preferences of customers, suppliers, and competitors, which when linked together suggest new ways to create value for them; selectively applies an array of past concepts or experiences to uncover value and impact in new contexts; and expands the scope of strategic thinking far into the future and far outside his or her own area. This level of insight allows an individual to attack high-value, high-complexity issues or opportunities that, if "solved" or "unlocked," can transform the business. It allows the person to recognize unquestioned assumptions of the business, and through exposing them, enables others to see new ways of doing things.

People who have a strongly developed trait of insight have a "tell" that will identify them to others: as soon as they seem to settle in, they are likely to move on to avoid getting bored. That's because they love learning new things that are aligned with their interests, things that are different from what they know already. In fact, it's the disparity among the components of their assembled knowledge that frequently becomes the hotbed for their insight. You will see this vividly in the experience of our case study subject for this chapter.

The Edge of Mark's Insight

The story of Mark Tercek is one that highlights the role and impact of insight across a career trajectory. Looking at his early career and into his current role as a leader in the sustainability movement, we can see the way his innate insight helped him routinely make critical choices and choose paths that deviated from the norm around him. Mark's lifelong use of insight as a guiding force demonstrates the relevance and power of this trait in both sustainability leadership and the creation of a culture of purpose.

Insight combines adaptation, exploration, instinct, and courage. It is also strongly rooted in an ongoing eagerness to learn. In the course of my conversations with Mark, he spoke often of moments of insight fueled by learning—whether a new skill or a new culture or a new way of conducting business. Mark also has a word he often uses to characterize his experiences: luck. You'll hear Mark say again and again that he was frequently lucky. But more often than not, it was luck of his own making—opportunity he was able to carve out for himself through a willingness to see the possibilities in many situations. If strategy is the craft of being consistently lucky, then insight is the art.

Although he could not have named it at the time, Mark's first experience with his own insight came when he was thirteen. Living in a working-class neighborhood in Cleveland, Mark was presented with an opportunity: a scholarship to attend a prestigious boarding school.

Few in his neighborhood of auto and steel workers thought this sounded like a good idea. But Mark had a feeling. "I had an intuition that going to boarding school was a good idea even though it was extraordinarily weird in my circles. None of us had even heard of boarding school. It seemed alien, and I had very mixed feelings about it. But it was an immediate fit. The stuff I was exposed to, the range of ideas—I felt like I had a lot in common with these people." The experience reinforced Mark's innate willingness to take a chance and leap into situations that would allow him to learn more, to grow—even in the face of seemingly significant risk.

Because insight is a trait that came naturally to Mark early in his life, he learned early on to trust and foster it. He called on it again as he graduated Harvard. While classmates gravitated to Wall Street and other corporate training grounds, Mark opted to travel to Japan.

"Going to Japan seemed like a really good idea. How could it be a bad idea?"

He took a job as an English teacher and began serious study of martial arts. His choice of aikido is telling. Aikido stresses mental training more than do most other martial arts. Practitioners focus on being relaxed under stress—just as insight relies on the ability to step back and see the bigger picture.

Mark's early career moves would take him back and forth between Japan and New York in the employ of Goldman Sachs. One New York assignment was as head of the transportation practice. "I was going to decline that job; it sounded so boring. My friends were all doing sexier things like technology, communications, financial services." But in the end he took the assignment. And it worked for him in large part because he brought his ability to see opportunity where others did not.

"I was able to make it not boring. There were roughly two categories of clients. There were transportation industry clients that already had Goldman Sachs relationships. Those teams wanted nothing to do with me because to the extent that there was business, they didn't want to share the credit. Then there were all the others where we were nowhere. What I concluded was that I would only be successful by aggressively sharing credit with others on any success I had. And I discovered that there was no penalty for sharing credit."

Seeing that his freely sharing credit with all those with whom he collaborated allowed others to gravitate to his team, he built on that discovery. "I would get praised for being so nice about sharing credit, but I was doing it on purpose because I needed help. So we had a tiny transportation team—just a few people. At one point, we had a very big business, but really the team was much bigger because we had all these products specialists and regional people working on our deals."

Soon afterwards, Mark became a partner and thought about what would be next for him. "The transportation orange didn't have much more juice really, and I was getting bored."

Thanks to an exit by another partner, Mark was offered a new opportunity. "I don't know if I was the fourth, fifth, or tenth person they thought of for the job, but on Thanksgiving, right after I became a partner, in 1996, I remember the call, and my bosses said, would you consider being the head of the Goldman Sachs real estate effort? I almost fell out of my chair," he says. He accepted on the spot. "The opportunity was big: to supervise eighty people, a $100 million business, much higher profile than transportation would ever be. In my mind I was thinking, 'Holy shit! You're going to be the head of the real estate group!'"

"I didn't even bother asking for advice. I just took it. I was so pumped, and I had a big group. I was really a leader and would learn more stuff! I was reporting to the heads of banking on my big business. I was making people decisions. It was fantastic," he says. And again, his instinct turned out to be an insight. "I was right about that hunch that I knew how to run stuff. Turns out I was better at that than the deal business. Hiring people, picking priorities, negotiating with opponents in the firm when there was trouble, and diplomatically doing things—all that leadership stuff. I was good at it."

One of his mentors at the time, Rob Kaplan (now the Martin Marshall Professor of Management Practice at the Harvard Business School), remembers Mark's evolution into a leader with impact. Rob had been Mark's boss at Goldman in Japan, where he had pushed him to step forward more: "Having insight on how to add value is great, but only if you act on it. Occasionally, that means making some waves. In Mark's case, on top of it, I knew he'd get bored if he wasn't challenged."

So far, you've seen Mark's insight serve Mark. But it is at this juncture in Mark's story where we see his insight begin to serve others—and, ultimately, the sustainable transformation of Mark's career and the companies he worked in.

Mark's personal sustainability transformation came during off hours—on vacation with his wife and children. He took every opportunity to bring his city-born children out into nature, creating interesting, active—or, as he described them, "geeky"—vacations. It was on these family adventures that he began to wonder if he had tapped out his trajectory as a banker, if he had anything new left to learn in this area of his professional life. A new idea began edging into his thought process: "I had this interest in the environment. It was extremely undeveloped," he says. "I was interested in business being a force for good."

Convinced he could not do that at Goldman, he prepared to leave. "When I told people I was going to quit, most of them said best of luck, don't let the door hit you on the way out. But [then CEO] Hank Paulson said, 'Don't quit. We need leaders like you.' It was really Hank who had the idea that I lead the firm's environmental effort. I thought it was kind of a weird idea, but he talked me into it."

Ironically, it was Paulson who quit to head the U.S. Treasury. But Mark stayed on to lead the environmental business. He began to develop strategies that made both business and environmental sense—a new concept in the halls of Goldman. "I was fearless, which was the most important ingredient. I had confidence. I had nothing to lose because I was otherwise going to quit. My insight was the realization that my clout in that job came from people remembering that I had been a pretty successful commercial guy. So that also told me that I needed to get stuff done quickly, because the bank does not remember stuff for a very long time. It was fun for me, and of course, I got world-class introduction to the environmental space."

Mark learned a lot, fast. One day, a headhunter called Mark looking for his insight: Could he suggest any good candidates for the job of heading The Nature Conservancy (TNC)? "And I said, yeah, I have a good idea—me."

Not everyone agreed that this idea was so good. "I had lunch with the chairman of the board of the World Wildlife Fund. I remember when I told him my plan to get the job at TNC, he very kindly brought me down to earth and helped me understand that while it might be a worthy idea, it was never going to happen."

But now practiced at trusting himself on career issues, Mark forged ahead. He knew that the onus was on him to make a compelling case for why a banker should be welcomed into this role. "So I prepared, like you would expect a diligent banker to prepare; I mean I prepared like crazy. We had a lot of Goldman Sachs people who were on TNC chapter boards, and I just grilled them. I really went nuts. I turned over every stone to prepare. "

Once he was in the interview room, Mark made a compelling case that the future would be different, that understanding deals, companies, and markets would become a key factor of success for NGOs in the twenty-first century. This insight differentiated his candidacy. It was a long, hard slog to convince TNC. But Mark was committed—this was the job he wanted. So much so that when the call finally came offering the job, he was so excited that he backed his car into a tree.

Insight had guided Mark through ambitious choices. It had helped him turn slow assignments into winners and inspired him to seek out a greater purpose for his work, even though many were unable to see how a banker could get a job like this. But now, Mark would take his own insight to its highest expression—to change the course of an organization committed to sustainability.

"When I arrived at TNC, I was trying to figure out how we paid for everything. I couldn't make sense of it. It seemed to me that we were spending more dollars than we were raising. It also seemed to me that we had way too many projects, and some were just subpar. I had only been there about a month and then Lehman Brothers went bust, and I knew we would have a financial crisis. Just knew it."

Mark had gone through a few downturns on Wall Street. He took what he learned to TNC. "We were by far the first environmental NGO to move. I proposed to the board that we lower our budget by $100 million, from $530 million to $430 million. They were shocked. They said, no, $100 million is too much. Lower by $80 million. But we ultimately did lower it by $100 million."

Mark noted that it was a stressful time, but it was a necessary change to an organization in pursuit of a demanding mission.

"Of course, one part of it was very hard—we had to ask some very good people to leave. We did that in the kindest way and were pleased that most of them landed on their feet, but it was tough." Because he saw the shape of things to come early on, TNC was able to grow stronger from the crisis. "Really, we would've had the problem without the financial crisis. We were living beyond our means. I think it turned out for me to be a great entry because it validated my leadership at a difficult time. Then, we executed very well. We had to fire people, and that's never fun. We executed that quickly. We became a highly prioritized and focused leaner organization and then we grew."

Because Mark knew how quickly the crisis could (and, indeed, did) unfold, he immediately instituted the first year of his five-year plan, even though at first, "the trustees hated it." But he brought them in, engaged them in the process, and ultimately secured their buy-in.

Mark then began to apply his prior training to his new role. He could see where the matrixed approach of the business world could serve as a buttress for this environmentally focused operation. "We used to be a region-based organization. We had all these individual regional units. They were all pretty damn good and mostly did their own thing. Life was simple. Now we have a new strategic plan where we are going to tackle the world's most complex challenges. To do that, it's not that simple anymore. I realized that the regions can't possibly know enough to solve these big problems locally."

"So I had to bring the right people to the right roles, as I had learned at Goldman in my transportation job. This means hiring some people, but it also means looking for talent within TNC and developing them. They have to run around the world scaling our strategy, get all these people in the regions doing stuff."

Insight does not imply an unbroken string of successes, and not every hunch played out as expected. Mark was confident, for example, that his leadership style honed at Goldman would be transferable to his new job. But that wasn't the case. "At Goldman, people like Hank and Rob are famously straightforward. To the point of being really off-putting and difficult. They call it the way they see it, and they don't pull their punches. I was like that at the beginning of TNC too, and I was wrong."

Mark realized that he was off to a bad start with a lot of people, overdoing candor and straightforwardness: "I was forgetting that the CEO is always in the spotlight. You have to give people reasons to be confident and hopeful. If you're having a bad day or you think somebody's idea is poor, you can't just say so, like I did at Goldman Sachs. So, I recognized that I needed to shift gears and change."

And Mark learned this new style of leadership as he transformed TNC into a best-in-class NGO. With that learning, again, came insight.

■ ■ ■

Mark's story shows us the full spectrum of insight. First, the trait implies the ability to draw on a breadth of experiences and distill patterns from their complexity. Mark actively constructed such a repository of experiences he could later draw on. As Goldman's first leader of the environmental business, Mark brought to bear his experience leading across geographies and across industries. Second, people with insight make a point of setting aside time to think big, integrating analytical and conceptual thinking. Mark did this on his own time during family vacations, but increasingly scaled his big idea until it became his job. Third, insight means constant learning and the ability to connect seemingly unrelated lessons by asking "what if" questions. We saw at several points in Mark's story his restlessness when he felt that he was no longer learning or applying what he had learned in novel settings, as he did in recognizing the looming financial crisis and preparing TNC with the same rigor he had applied in banking.

Understanding the Person: Markers for the Trait of Insight

Insight can be an understated trait, but it is critical throughout the organization because experiences can vary widely between the core and the frontier of your business. You want people

148

at every station capable of bringing the full diversity of their backgrounds to thinking deeply about what they are doing, why they are doing it, and how it relates to the purpose of the organization as a whole. Some of the most important challenges and awesome opportunities of the years ahead will be visible to others in your organization long before you can spot them. If they have insight, it will make all the difference.

Whereas some imbued with it will have a lightbulb moment in a public way, many more will simply see connections to places visited, voices heard, and things seen, and draw conclusions while quietly going about their business. These are people you want to bring into your culture and encourage to shine. The following questions will help you identify the most insightful people as you hire into your organization.

What to Look For	How to Look for It
These individuals ask heretical questions (and make irreverent choices) that sidestep commonly held assumptions.	What idea are you most proud of for overcoming skepticism and changing the direction of a group of people?
	Tell me about a time you followed your instinct with little other evidence.
They are conceptual thinkers who can oscillate between the nuanced and the big picture.	What is the most interesting idea you have come across this month? What makes that idea interesting?
	When did a seemingly innocuous external stimulus lead you to an epiphany?

What to Look For	How to Look for It
They have a track record of recycling disparate experiences and applying them in nonintuitive settings.	What are the similarities between these two seemingly disparate areas of your life (for example, aikido and running an NGO)? When were you most surprised to see something you had learned turn up again in a new setting?
They get bored as soon as they feel they have stopped learning.	Walk me through your job changes in the past and explain what made you switch. When was the last time you got bored with your job, and what did you do about it?
They more intuitively see possibility where others see risk.	What is an example of a widely feared risk you have disregarded? What was the upside you were after? Where were you lucky in your life, and why do you suppose that was?
They are open to learning from nearly every possible source.	When have others helped you see a problem from a different angle and rethink it? Who was the most surprising source of information for you last month?

Red Flags: People lacking insight tend to think through issues from a narrow perspective. They get stuck in accustomed thinking patterns and rely on past assumptions, rather than asking "what if" questions. In dealing with complex data, they will focus on what they already know rather than grappling with the unknown or ambiguous. In referencing them, you are less likely to run across mentors or thought partners who helped them stretch their thinking.

Staying Hungry with Curiosity

Neil deGrasse Tyson is the director of the Hayden Planetarium at the American Museum of Natural History, and his home is littered with broken stuff, mostly toys and other small objects his children have explored and dismantled. But Neil is not disturbed by the collateral damage. As far as he's concerned, it's curiosity at its best. Curiosity is a trait he admires and embraces in his own work as a scientist. "A scientist is a child who has never grown up," he tells me. "They will always poke and probe and test and do an experiment. Even if it's at risk of breaking something."

Because curiosity is a trait, it imbues everything Neil has done. He studied physics at Harvard, while also rowing and wrestling on the varsity team. By the time he earned his doctorate in astrophysics, he had also become a national gold medalist in Latin ballroom dance. Whether publishing statistical analysis of U.S. presidential elections, testifying in front of the

U.S. Senate, or discussing the importance of empathy with PETA, Neil goes where his curiosity takes him.

"The innovation of most famous ideas comes about because someone brings the fruits of curiosity from some other field," says Neil. "Another way of thinking, some kind of brain wiring they brought to bear on their discovery." But, as Neil admits with a smile, these are accidents. "The trick is to have enough accidents to come up with some good ideas."[1]

His curiosity is not primarily directed toward collecting knowledge to solve another problem; it's a trait that makes him ask questions about the world as he perceives it. "We stand on the brink of great discoveries," Neil says. "And we always will, as long as we keep exploring."

Curiosity

Curiosity is the secret sauce of a culture of purpose. You can spot it in every chapter of this book, and it is in fact prominently present throughout the journeys of companies on the path to sustainability. Without it, nothing goes.

Curiosity means seeking. Seeking out new experiences, ideas, and knowledge, but also seeking feedback and changing behavior in response to it. Curious people break stuff. They do it literally, such as by trying to figure out how that asymmetrical vase balances. They do it figuratively—for example, by demoting Pluto from planethood, as Neil deGrasse Tyson did (to the dismay of countless schoolkids). They are always learning, and taking what they have learned in different areas to apply it to new ones. They will look around your office and start asking about stuff.

Curiosity is not always clean or pretty. The most curious people won't think twice about disregarding many of the structures and hierarchies that have propelled today's leaders to their roles. They'll ask difficult questions at inopportune moments in public forums. They'll raise new issues just as everything seems wrapped up. They'll take it upon themselves to try out a new process or theory without asking permission or even alerting anyone first. This is why failing is an essential activity in a culture of purpose. More specifically, sustainability means accepting the certainty of frequent small and cheap failures at the frontier (fueled by curiosity) to ward off the potential company killer at the core (fueled by adherence to the status quo). As you will see in the chapter on openness, a culture supportive of curiosity should maximize the ease of correcting mistakes rather than the difficulty of making them.

On the flipside, curious people are less likely to default to prior knowledge in seeking to explaining novel situations. Take, for instance, our innate preference for explaining the behavior of others with reasons that are personality based rather than situational. It's called the *fundamental attribution error* (FAE), and it is particularly common in Western culture.[2] I might more likely assume, for example, that the person who did not hold the elevator for me is a dolt rather than that he's late for an interview. Curious people are less likely to commit FAEs and more likely to ask questions and understand a particular situation.

Curiosity comprises two broad characteristics. The first has to do with the extent to which the individual is open to new experience and input. You may have heard the saying that specialists learn more and more about less and less until they know everything about nothing, while generalists learn less and less about more and more until they know nothing about everything. True curiosity will tend to favor the generalist side of the spectrum, because people with this trait are intrigued by any number of things. Contrast this to determination (discussed in Chapter Seven), which is closer to the specialist's side. Curious people, in other words, will go wide or go deep at various points, simply based on what's most interesting to them at that moment. It is worth noting that dopamine, long linked to the brain's pleasure and reward centers, is now known to cause seeking behavior. The dopamine system, in other words, causes us to desire, to search—and it gets stimulated by the unpredictable.[3] Curious people are always itching for their next dopamine hit.

That is only half the story, however. You are also looking for a second characteristic: the desire not just to look and understand, but also to learn and change as a consequence—to adapt. So it is learning, together with awareness and openness, that is at the heart of this trait.

What are the indicators that an individual possesses this critical trait? You can see it in his or her everyday actions. When I first met Jochen Zeitz, then CEO of PUMA, he told me about the moment he took over the company in 1993. Jochen's view of sustainability was that it is "the most important investment you can make in your business." But in 1993, PUMA had no money, and Jochen's focus had to be squarely on getting the company to survive. But even then, he says, he "wondered about the

154

impact of PUMA's raw material needs on the environment" and "scratched my head how we could help create a more peaceful and more creative world." That is why as soon as PUMA could afford it, Jochen started to measure stuff, from supplier metrics to inventory data, to understand what actually moved the needle, and to question the assumptions the company had taken for granted. Many of those assumptions—for example, that the PUMA brand would never work for women—were false. His objective was not to prove others wrong; it was to learn. From anybody. "You have to stop being so defensive. Looking away does not protect us—so let's find out. Rather than having a hard shell around us, we have to start engaging, asking, and learning. If you do, it will be a gold rush of innovation."

When you evaluate a leader for the trait of curiosity, observe her overall outlook first. Does this person seek out new experiences, ideas, knowledge? Has she decided to learn to knit or play the banjo? Does the individual proactively seek feedback and change her behavior in response? If she becomes aware that other banjo players struggle with her impatience, for example, and begins to meditate in response, that is a good indication of curiosity.

What does this curiosity look like in practice? At low but emerging levels of curiosity, the individual is open to learning and change, listens to and accepts input from others, and changes when needed. At a middle range, this trait becomes more noticeably active. The individual asks for help to learn and change, perceives others' reactions, and invites input from friends and valued people. The individual is willing to improve and adopts ideas from primarily within the organization or from prior experience. At its highest levels, curiosity becomes a driving force for change and exploration. This individual is energized by learning and change. He or she enthusiastically seeks to understand perspectives of colleagues at all levels of the organization, assumes there is value in what each person knows, and is interested in discovering how things could work better. The person brings together people who have different experiences and perspectives so as to test hypotheses and deepen understanding, and encourages disagreement with ideas to see how others' perspectives could enhance his or her own. This person takes a thought leadership position, but openly admits mistakes and sees them as a learning opportunity; establishes partners to constantly challenge his or her own assumptions, beliefs, and self-image; is aware of his or her own areas of development; and adapts.

The Primacy of Curiosity

All the attributes of a culture of purpose rely on the curiosity of its people. It is the energy that powers the mind to ask, "How come it works that way? How could it be entirely different?" Most everyone I've talked to stepped from a place of relative calm into the turmoil and potential of change—for many individual and unique reasons, but also for one common one: out of curiosity.

This is why I will look at curiosity through a variety of lenses. You'll see the trait brought to light by individuals you've already met in these pages. It's a good way to show how intertwined curiosity is with sustainable leadership and the building of a culture of purpose at any stage.

The story of Mark Tercek, in Chapter Eight, is one of a career trajectory marked by curiosity. At more than one time in his professional life, Mark came to a fork in the road, looked hard at the less-traveled choice, and wondered: What would that be like? What could be the downside of trying this unusual thing?

Rather than allowing curiosity to push past his comfort zone, it actually widened that comfort zone and enabled Mark to travel farther afield, hungry for new experiences.

The phrase "How could it be a bad idea?" has become a refrain in Mark's career whenever his curiosity gets the better of him. After completing his MBA and going to work for Goldman Sachs, for example, Mark's employer wanted him to return to Japan.

"Then, 100 percent of my internal advisers, my friends and mentors, said this is a bad idea. Backwater; not much business there; shouldn't give up your clients. But I said, well, that may all be true, so maybe there is some risk, but on the other hand, how cool! Why not try it?"

It is Mark's coursing thread of curiosity that guided him forward at each step in his career. It would happen again and again. He would see opportunities in sleepy divisions of Goldman—opportunities that others could not perceive but that he was intrigued by and willing to dig out and make shine. As he became more senior, he began to synthesize the values he held in his personal life with the work he was doing—and became curious about ways to connect those two worlds. His concern that his children could grow up in

157

a world without nature made him wonder: What could I be doing in my work that would benefit the natural world for my family? This quest for understanding propelled him into a leadership role at Goldman's environmental effort and then, in a leap that seemed outlandish to observers, led him to apply for and get the job as head of The Nature Conservancy.

It's just not commonplace to see a Goldman banker turn up at the head of a leading nonprofit. The ability to envision that possibility calls for a strong sense of personal curiosity: What could be bad about that? How risky could that be?

To the curious, not very.

Incorporating Curiosity

Personal curiosity is just one way this trait manifests. In previous chapters, you saw individuals who were able to stoke curiosity on a corporate level: What could happen if the company changed its ways? What very new and different process might we engage in as a business entity that would make the world better?

It was this corporate curiosity that you saw run through the story of Curtis Ravenel at Bloomberg. When a brief window presented itself to think big, Curtis stepped back and asked himself what his company might look like in the next quarter century. You'll notice that his thinking was increasingly unconstrained and led him to add fundamentally new services to the company's offerings, which in turn facilitated the rise of new kinds of investors. "Bloomberg loves information," Curtis says. "Information is our business; we are good at getting it. And what could be better than figuring out what our business will look like ten years from now?"

This kind of curiosity requires a certain irreverence, which can cause discomfort at the corporate level. Even the presence of leeway does not imply the absence of discomfort. Curiosity leads into the unknown, and at least some of the unknown is not what you had in mind.

All Together Now

Finally, let's look at curiosity and its role on the grander scale of creating a culture of purpose. To recognize the driving force of sustainability in the world we live in, we must call on the power of curiosity. To pursue sustainability as a commercial opportunity and strategic imperative demands it. Why? Because sustainability remains unclaimed territory across vast tracts of the business world. Even embracing the role of sustainable change agent in a corporate setting calls for a creative and questioning outlook.

In many ways, Frank O'Brien-Bernini articulates this best in his discussion of the role he found himself in at Owens Corning. "Every day is something new playing in the field of sustainability or leading a company toward it," he says. "Because it's such a new C-level position, there are really no rules, and so every day you've got to decide where you're going to put your energy and where you can make a difference." One day, that might be working with the salespeople to convert a builder of coal-fueled housing to zero-net-energy buildings. The next, it could be working with an environmental organization in attaining incentives to launch a renewable project.

The day after that, it could be a fuel-switching project at one of the company's plants.

Frank reflects: "You can occupy yourself with a million different things, but trying to figure it out—that's the good bit. I think often of the plate-spinning guy—your job is not to keep spinning a plate, but it's to pick which one to get going." Curiosity fuels his ongoing search for a new challenge—the next plate to spin. But, importantly, he also created a means for others at Owens Corning to start asking questions. By setting up the capital fund and spurring employees throughout the organization to offer their best ideas, Frank made curiosity a privilege of the culture itself.

What would it take for the company to get five, ten, fifteen other suppliers to reduce their footprint? What's the next big thing that should happen inside the company's own plants? How can clients—builders and architects—accelerate change in the community? "What will it take? Where's the best place to start?" Frank asks, "I don't know if it's ever done!" What he does know, however, is that the questions are as endless as the opportunities, and many of the best ones will be asked by others.

And this sense of wonder is perhaps the most important way curiosity manifests for our discussion. To create a culture of purpose, one must be curious about it all—wondering what is possible, what stakeholders will have to say, what might happen if different groups were to exchange knowledge and set big goals. It is curiosity that powers all of the competencies we've discussed. To the curious mind the possibilities for change are endless and exhilarating.

Understanding the Person: Markers for the Trait of Curiosity

First and foremost, curiosity assumes there is a better way. In rejecting the notion that things are as good as they get, this trait forces a continuous evolution throughout a culture. Many small mutations, driven by curious people throughout, lead to a more adaptive and nimble organization. Second, curiosity means seeking and learning from new information, including negative feedback. That means discomfort is built into the experience—but also excitement, inspiration, and fun. Third, curiosity encourages both transparency and conflict. It requires me to ask questions about the things I don't know and embrace sources of information that run counter to what I do know.

A leader who maximizes the number of curious people in her organization has achieved a great deal. But it's easier said than done. Hiring people with this trait means getting comfortable with being uncomfortable. Curiosity eschews control and breeds irreverence: Your title and seniority will matter less. You'll be interrupted more. But in the long run, it will beat the alternative hands down.

When looking for your most curious high-potential performers, start in the principal's office, or the corporate version thereof. The curious have been sent there often. They poke around where they're not meant to be, they dig into questions and problems that others see as unimportant, they dismantle, they quiz, they surprise you on a regular basis. In many ways, curiosity is the king of traits—it is the powering force that makes possible all of the competencies in Part One. Without it, an individual may find the challenge daunting. With it, the challenge is irresistible.

There is no role in your organization that does not benefit from curiosity, and the following questions help detect the trait as you bring on new talent.

What to Look For	How to Look for It
These individuals have an underdeveloped respect for both sacred cows and risk.	When have you gotten in trouble for disregarding a cultural norm? What's the last thing you did that truly scared you?
They have imported novel ways of thinking with surprising outcomes.	Where have you found a past experience to be unexpectedly relevant in a new setting? Outside school and work, where have you learned the most?
They can get distracted by what happens to be most interesting to them.	When have you stumbled on a topic that completely captivated you for a while? Good of you to ask about the broadsword hanging in my office. What do you make of it?
They find it more rewarding to learn from others than to prove them wrong.	What motivation do you get from learning, seeking out different experiences, and reaching out to others for new ideas? When did you last do so? How do you go about meeting people who will challenge your assumptions, beliefs, and self-image?
They are not defensive.	Do you proactively seek developmental feedback? What have you learned? What has been your favorite failure?

162

What to Look For	How to Look for It
They have a sense of optimism and wonder.	What everyday thing or event has most recently amazed you, and why?
	What would you like to be true at the end of your career that is not true already?

Red Flags: Incurious people as a rule do not seek "expert" opinions or disconfirming evidence. They may not willfully avoid doing so, as they can lack awareness of their own developmental areas, although they tend to be uncomfortable sharing mistakes. In referencing them, you will probably find that they are uncomfortable raising controversial issues and have repeatedly closed off dialogues with points of view differing from their own.

PART 3

Building a Culture of Purpose

In 1971, the psychologist Philip Zimbardo conducted what has become known as the Stanford Prison Experiment. Zimbardo randomly separated two dozen students into prisoners and guards in a mock prison environment and observed their (d)evolving behavior. After six days, a culture of psychological abuse had grown so pervasive that Zimbardo was forced to terminate the experiment.[1]

Leaders have the opportunity to promote the right behaviors by creating a rather different environment. More than that, they have an obligation to do so, beginning with taking ownership of the beliefs and customs that shape their organization. As we have seen in the first two parts of this book, the tools at your disposal include promoting the right people to lead change and hiring the right new people to accelerate it. Both of these reflect your ability to choose the right people. But what about making the right people choose your organization?

Bonding together the people of your organization, their ways of thinking and behaving, is their collective culture. And changing culture is hard. But if the right people join you and share in a purpose that motivates them, your organization will be difficult to stop.

In Part Three, I address the broader attributes a culture of purpose needs to thrive. These are the cultural attributes that must be fostered and modeled by leadership, so that others can amplify them throughout the organization. They are also the first things you will be asked about by the best candidates and future leaders. The foundation of these attributes is the purpose itself, the leitmotif endowing the organization with alignment of intent.

Energy

When Matthew VanBesien is in a hurry, he does not wait for the elevator. He bounds up the stairs to his office. On the sixth floor. And as executive director of the New York Philharmonic, Matthew is in a hurry a lot, because he is in the business of managing a high-energy culture.

The New York Philharmonic has given over fifteen thousand performances—a milestone unsurpassed by any other orchestra in the world. Its uniformly world-class musicians, numbering over one hundred, play an average of 150 home performances a year. When you factor in the rehearsing that goes into this blistering pace, along with another couple dozen performances on the road in unprecedented locations like Pyongyang, a simple question arises: How can the energy for such a routine be sustained when excellence cannot be compromised?

Speaking with Matthew, I took away three points. First, he says, bring on the very best people, no matter how difficult it is. Indeed, nearly every musician performing in this ensemble was recognized as a child prodigy and won a daunting set of awards before he or she had the opportunity to audition. The very best people want to be surrounded by the very best people, because they have learned that what they can do together is addictively good. Second, understand what the orchestra is capable of, and design a schedule that stays on the right side of the line. This is a difficult and multivariate task, taking into account not only the familiarity with and complexity of new pieces to be performed (and the halls that host them, from Adelaide to Zurich), but also the dynamics of the performers individually and collectively. These performers thrive on being challenged—that's what made them great. The trick is to provide the challenge at a level that allows the orchestra to experience flow[1] rather than anxiety or boredom. Finally, allow the musicians to decompress in whatever way they choose, and keep an eye on their collective state of mind. These are professionals, after all, who develop their own routines to perform at this level. Among them are Fulbright scholars, instrument builders, and Grammy Award winners, and when they are not on stage, they do not lack for activity.

Matthew's description expanded on an idea that Yvon Chouinard, founder of Patagonia, told me once: the secret of Patagonia is to "hire great people and leave them alone."[2] When I asked Matthew how he keeps track of the energy of the orchestra, he shared a story of a performance they gave at Carnegie Hall. The schedule preceding this concert, which was to be a piece by Mahler that they had not played in a while, allowed only one practice the day of the performance.

Matthew was in the audience, of course, and he heard that "it was not perfect," quickly adding that "it was nothing most people would pick up, but it was there." The reason that Matthew relaxed the schedule in the following year was not just that the quality expectation of the New York Philharmonic is so high, but that he knows that this expectation is nowhere higher than among the musicians themselves. Performances below that level frustrate these professionals and deplete their energy. Matthew says simply, "My job is to provide the best possible environment for the orchestra to perform to their full potential."

High-Energy Cultures

Energy describes the degree to which a culture self-starts and maintains long-term momentum at a high level. It's the mojo of your tribe. It implies a special kind of motivation—an ambition to be successful as a fully engaged team. High-energy cultures reinforce themselves by continuously gauging team motivation and pressure points. They provide feedback to support feelings of engagement with the group and the task at hand.

Energy is the leading cultural trait and primary ingredient as companies begin to build a culture of purpose. In fact, where the energy of a culture has fallen short, leaders who cannot re-ignite that spark will fail. How energized is the culture by collaboration? How proactive is the organization as a whole? How ably does it sustain momentum? Cultures can fall into three energy categories: Low energy describes a passive culture—one that needs external prodding to ooze slightly faster. In the middle range, you would find a culture responsive and able to act when things need to be done. But at the high end of this scale, you'll find the transformative players.

A high-energy culture is exceptionally productive, proactive, and action oriented over a long period of time. These are the cultures that will drive transformative, sustainable change in a company or industry, and even on a global scale. Think of a high-energy culture as a beehive, the symbol of industriousness enshrined in coats of arms throughout history. Bees are highly affiliative; they have a strong shared objective and work relentlessly to achieve it—individually and collectively. They are abuzz, literally, and they Just. Won't. Quit.

Bob Sparks Shared Energy

Recognizing strong, high-energy teams is one thing. Creating them is another. Bob Kidder has made a career in corporate transformation and has imbued several cultures with energy along the way. He has demonstrated this ability across industries and decades. What's more, a look back at his work makes clear that he led sustainable transformations at the corporate level long before sustainability was in common parlance. To understand and learn from him, let's look at his work at three global firms: Duracell, Borden, and Chrysler. Each stop in Bob's career is a study in the creation of high-energy cultures.

When Bob arrived at Duracell in 1980, he found a company spending energy on a lot of internal bickering. In the company's European operations, he found the players acting out a variety of intercontinental debates. If it involved critiquing "corporate," people were doing it.

"I found a constant battle going on between headquarters and any one of the subsidiaries when I was in Europe. It could have been France; it could have been Belgium, Italy, Spain—it did not matter," he says. The direction of research, the strategy for marketing—this pervasive mood encompassed much, and it sucked a great deal of energy out of the organization. Bob's first step was to work at stopping it such that the participants could see the value of changing their fractious ways.

"I had them get together—all these country guys and the people in the European headquarters. And I did it with a conference I titled "Those Bastards." We didn't tell them the title until they arrived, but that's exactly what we called the meeting: Those Bastards. When people walked in the room, we had a horn sitting on the desk, with a big rubber bulb."

Bob laughs at the recollection. "So everybody had one of these in front of them. I started off by saying, 'You all can see a horn is sitting in your desk. What I want you to do is every time you are thinking to yourself *Those bastards!* squeeze the horn. I do not want you to sit there steaming; I want you to squeeze the horn and tell what is going on in your head: those bastards are doing it to me again. We need to get a good dialogue going about this.'"

Bob got a lot of laughs. And, throughout the meeting, a good bit of honking. But the tactic diffused the tension and made it possible to move into a more productive use of company energy. "We talked obviously about what was needed to unify the way we thought about ourselves and to get everybody pulling on the same chain," Bob says. This experience matches what we know about human behavior in a realm called *realistic conflict theory*. A 1950 experiment divided a group of eleven-year-old boys into two arbitrary subgroups, which then were separated to bond among themselves. When the two groups were reunited after one week, conflict ensued and worsened. Tellingly, the most effective way of overcoming this conflict was tasking both groups to solve a problem together—in other words, to "pull on the same chain."[3]

For Bob, that was just the first step toward reconfiguring the Duracell culture into an aligned culture of high energy. It was the first of many times he would meet with small groups, divisions, and individuals to work to break the cycle of unnecessary sniping, and redirect everyone toward the larger company goal.

Although he had trained that muscle in Europe, the moment to fully flex it arrived when he became CEO of the global company just before turning forty. It was time, he knew, to jolt the full company into the high-energy culture it was ready to become. Bob achieved this aim by unifying Duracell around the concept of "Duracell Best Design." Going into this transformational period, Bob was leading a company with multiple designs and manufacturing processes for what should have been a single product—the longest-lasting alkaline battery. That, he decided, would be the focal point of his mandate.

"There had been, from the time I was in Europe to the time I got back to the U.S., a kind of debate about whose product was the best. Was it the battery made in Europe, or was it the product made in the U.S.? This constant internal battle was draining, and we had not had the chutzpah to deal with it because of the politics behind the positions," he says.

Bob decided this would be the defining moment. He gathered his troops.

We were all sitting in the room and said let's figure out what we were going to do. At the end of the day, and this was a day-long discussion, there was nothing. There was no decision. And so I said, "Time-out. Stop. This discussion is over. First: we are going to have Duracell Best Design around the world, period. That decision is now made, and it means we are in the business of building the same longest-lasting batteries everywhere we compete. Second: we are going to get together and figure out what the Duracell Best Design is, and we need an outcome of that discussion within three months and a plan to implement the Duracell Best Design within three years everywhere. And finally: country management not producing the Duracell Best Design will no longer make product and will import it from countries that do. As leaders of the Duracell team, you need to continue the meeting and begin the planning on how to achieve Duracell Best Design." And I walked out.

Bob recalls the stunned silence as he got up and walked out of the room. "People were thinking, 'What did he just say?'"

But the message sank in as the door closed behind him. And it worked. Jolted from their persistent and circular debating, the team found its forward momentum. Bob had raised the stakes, and his team was energized by the clarity of what was to come.

Left with authority and marching orders, the Duracell team stepped up. A Duracell Best Design was designed, developed, and implemented. (Interestingly, the design was one that had as its core property the promise of longer battery life; it was a more sustainable product before anyone was really talking about sustainability.)

One of the great benefits of high-energy culture is that when engaged, it does not stop at the borders of any one team or project. It spills out into the company at large, and Bob ensured that by making every employee an equity owner in Duracell.

Bob described how it felt when energy took hold of Duracell:

When you make a decision like that, it ripples through the company nearly instantaneously. It got through the organization in a heartbeat, and there was just a different attitude afterwards. I made one decision, Duracell Best Design. But tens of thousands of other decisions were then made throughout the organization, which I had absolutely nothing to do with. And they all had the same goal—the longest-lasting product in the marketplace. It led to less material in the battery jacket, to better temperature control in the warehouse, to innovations ranging from a better morphology of zinc to integrated testers at the point of purchase. Duracell is a story of good people who needed a jolt and some decisive leadership.

Bob's description of decisions rippling through the organization and creating a different attitude reminded me of the phenomenon of *collective effervescence*, the perceived energy formed by people gathering at carnivals and raves (or riots).[4] Duracell, a company selling energy to consumers, was itself energized. Along the way, it became the market leader.

Accountability

In 1995, Bob agreed to steward another turnaround. It wasn't until he arrived that he fully understood the extent of the company's problems and the need for a jolt of energy.

Borden was a company with a balance sheet full of problems. Sustainability, in its case, had the most basic and immediate meaning: keeping the business going and figuring out paths to value. It had been acquired by the private equity powerhouse KKR, and KKR needed a leader it could trust to bring new energy to Borden in a hurry. The company was losing in the neighborhood of $200 million a year, and the question was how to make the best of a challenging situation. Bob came on originally to help on the acquisition due diligence and eventually was convinced by some friends to bring his expertise to the CEO job.

Bob spent his first month on the job observing the different businesses under the Borden umbrella. At the end of the thirty days, it was clear to him that Borden had, at its core, a cultural problem.

"There was no accountability—from anybody. There was a lot of 'I didn't do that' and 'It's not me,'" he says. "That was true no matter where you went in the company. Headquarters personnel blamed the guys in the field; the guys in the field blamed headquarters—no one took responsibility." A combination of weak leadership, insufficient energy focused on the business difficulties, and cultural confusion was at the root of the Borden performance problem.

To energize Borden by restoring accountability, Bob launched an initiative called "Taking Ownership." With senior management backing, he created LBOs within the LBO[5]: He set up Elmer's as a separate company; same with the chemicals company, the wallpaper company, the pasta company. He mapped out how Borden would reorganize and capitalize each one of those businesses separately, setting up each one with its own boards and directors. In every case, the people in the companies were to own some of the equity, as a way to have them take ownership both literally and figuratively.

Bob says, "So if you're the guy who was appointed the head of Elmer's, I would say to you, 'Ron, you are now the CEO of that business. Here is who is on your board. If you want to have all your people wear green shoes, that's fine with me. If you want to have different practices, that's fine, too; you just have to go through the board to approve like any other company would. You now control all of the Elmer's resources needed to manage your business.'"

176

In control and fully accountable: that's how it went, down the Borden line. There were CEOs of lots of businesses. Even the litigation attorney of Borden became a CEO—"CEO of the Tail," to be precise—inheriting an array of disparate stuff, from season tickets for the Dallas Cowboys to environmental liabilities. Because he wanted everybody to feel accountable, Bob said to the tail CEO: "Here is your package of responsibilities. I want you to figure out how you'll make the company money on this tail by reducing the liabilities or selling the assets. Take ownership!" He reflects and adds, "And she loved her job!"

In this way, each section of Borden was stripped of its ability to finger-point and deny responsibility. Leaders became accountable; they owned everything that happened under their watch. It was nearly exactly the opposite of Duracell, but in both cases the organization was jolted. Perhaps the most memorable example came from human resources. "We created a company called Borden Services. We gave it a board, made the head of HR its CEO, and guaranteed a one-year supply agreement to provide their payroll and benefit administration to all these companies we had just created. At the end of that year, Borden companies were free to source all of their HR services anywhere. And Borden Services did well." So well, in fact, that they not only supported Borden's businesses but also began to serve companies outside of Borden. Eventually, another company came along and made a bid for Borden Services. Borden got some cash and saved $20 million of severance for what originally had been regarded simply as a corporate function with no sense of ownership.

At Borden, with accountability came energy. When your job is your responsibility, you are able to summon the energy to be great.

Speed

This brings us to Chrysler, the most recent recipient of an energy upgrade. Bob became chairman when the automaker entered bankruptcy. The Chrysler bankruptcy reflected a quarter century of bureaucratic decision making and a decade of governance turmoil.

Duracell was energized by a shared mission and Borden by a sense of accountability. Chrysler needed the energy to embrace something else to reinvigorate its brand: risk-taking.

Chrysler, Bob says, was burdened by the shackles of the industry and internal bureaucracy. There were lingering scars from the unhappy period of Daimler's ownership. The lack of alignment between the owners and the people running the company slowed things down and reduced the willingness to take risk.

In place of energy, bureaucracy had set in. "You had to go through four layers with a PowerPoint presentation that was different at each level. By the time it went up and came back down to the level of the guy who was making the proposal, the idea was watered down. Not only that, but it took a long time. It just sapped the energy out of the organization, and it really slowed the place down, really slowed life," Bob says.

As chairman, Bob selected and assembled the board of directors for the new Chrysler—not the Chrysler that had filed for bankruptcy protection, but the one that would emerge from it. But he is quick to point out that the company's new CEO, Sergio Marchionne, and his management team did the heavy lifting of Chrysler's transformation. Not surprisingly, when Bob early on suggested to Sergio a day on the racetrack to energize the board, the decision was instant. And indeed Sergio and his board bonded during a high-octane day driving cars on the Chrysler test track.

Bob noted Sergio's effect on culture at Chrysler. "Sergio just crashed through it on day one." Bob was aware that Sergio was known to engage directly with employees, and immediately upon arriving at Chrysler (visibly the antithesis of bureaucracy in his trademark sweater rather than a suit), he lived up to his reputation by moving the CEO's office from the penthouse to the middle of the engineering department.

Sergio set out to clean house and keep in the ranks only those managers willing to embrace a new era of risk-taking at Chrysler. Sergio knew what was going on in the company, and he was focused on selecting the right people to get the company back on track. Bob describes it: "Being smart, accountable, and respected by others at Chrysler—those were Sergio's primary criteria." Functional expertise mattered less.

Sergio overhauled the senior leadership and ended up with fifteen direct reports, most of whom had two functions. So the guy who had design also had Dodge. The guy who had Ram also led sales, and so forth. Bob says: "Suddenly, we had this very flat organization, and guess what? The speed picked up immensely because Sergio is very decisive." Risk-taking also increased, as Sergio gave his managers true authority. Sergio,

Bob recalls, gave clear directions and then full authority to take risks without bureaucratic barriers. And because he had fifteen direct reports at Chrysler—and more than that at Fiat—it was clear that he would not, indeed could not, micromanage. People had to make smart decisions and be accountable. Energy began rippling through Chrysler.

"He was relentless about commitments, so in terms of culture, it was about speed and risk-taking. I don't think Sergio ever labeled it such, but that's what it was. If you think about Eminem's "8 Mile Road"—it's an anthem about taking risk. You only get one chance to take advantage of it. That was the anthem for the company. You get one chance, and we need to make this company successful." That song, of course, became the background to Chrysler's Super Bowl commercials.

When Chrysler paid back their debt in early 2011, Bob received a plaque commemorating the event with a quotation: "I am only interested in the future because that is where I intend to spend the rest of my life." That quotation, derived from one coined by Charles Kettering a century earlier, captures the central idea of creating a sustainable culture.

Tellingly, as the company was nearing the point of paying back the government loan early, Sergio Marchionne sent out an email to all Chrysler employees redefining sustainability, no longer as a matter of immediate survival, but as one of shaping the future in which all of them would spend the rest of their lives. Here are the final paragraphs of the memo describing where sustainability meets a culture of purpose:

The choice we have is between seeking only to build up our own organization, or to develop a profitable enterprise that also promotes a better world. For my part, the choice is clear. The only way I can look at myself in the mirror every morning is if I know that sustainability is part of the very fabric of our business, and that we are helping create the conditions on which a positive future can emerge for our company, our children and humanity as a whole.

Our success will be judged not only by what we do, but by how it is achieved. This is a responsibility that will challenge us every day, but will ultimately lend deeper significance to who and what we are.

In his vision for the future of this company, Sergio Marchionne described a culture of purpose. Energy was fundamental to that culture's birth and will remain key to its sustained success.

■ ■ ■

Because cultures are energized by the act of collaborating, shared momentum itself is valuable. We saw that high-energy cultures, first, have the courage to halt everything, take stock, and then restart. When Bob gathered his executive team at Duracell and allowed them to jostle for a full day before laying down the law, he was counting on the cultural whiplash to rip people out of business-as-usual mode. Second, energy must be recognized as a strategic asset and fiercely protected. This is what Bob did by setting up fully autonomous businesses under the Borden Group and allowing each to create and guard its own way of doing things. Third, people in high-energy cultures love working together, and Chrysler's assembling the fifteen

181

most respected people into an executive team aims to create precisely such an environment.

Understanding the Culture: Markers for the Attribute of Energy

As a leader, you have enormous control over the energy that permeates your organization. And you want it to be high. You want people to be so excited to be a part of your organization that they get speeding tickets on the way into the office and still want to talk about their work over dinner. The phrase "bringing out the best in people" is used by a lot of organizations, but the truth is that in a high-energy culture, people themselves bring their best because it makes them feel great.

When looking for cultural attributes, look all over. Culture displays itself in the way individuals move through the halls, in the stories they tell, the places they gather, the successes and failures they catalogue. Energy is an attribute you can see in any meeting. Does the room buzz? Is action a given? Does it feel like it drags on forever or just got started? Energy will not stay hidden. If it's there, you'll feel it. The following questions are designed to gauge the energy of an organizational culture.

What to Look For	How to Look for It
The organization knows what it is capable of.	When has the infrastructure of this company felt most stretched?
	What are the big, hairy goals of this company, and how are you doing in reaching them?
People have the space to decompress.	What do you do when you are not here? Are there company sports teams?

What to Look For	How to Look for It
Leaders ensure that people voice their views (with a bullhorn if necessary).	Are there mechanisms for exchange, such as animated town hall gatherings or skip-level meetings? What topic is being most hotly debated across the company right now?
Once voices have been heard, the organization converges toward a shared direction.	What's an example of a topic the organization has only recently gelled around? What's your view of that?
People take ownership of that shared direction into their own areas and take initiative.	Are people throughout the organization empowered to take risks? What risks are you taking? What kinds of things are you working on simply because you want to?
Decisions are made quickly and transparently.	How do decisions get made here? What big decision did you have a voice in? How did it happen?
Leaders are genuinely respected throughout the organization.	Do people get 360-degree feedback? Where is the leadership team strongest?
The culture has aspirations.	What is the most extraordinary thing this company has done since you joined? What's next?

Red Flags: You will intuitively spot the greatest challenge to energy. It's the paralysis of a debating society: as soon as alignment arises, new arguments are brought up (the genesis of Bob's defining moment at Duracell). The culture tolerates too much complexity. Trade-offs necessary to reach a decision are either not accepted outright or devolved through the corporate hierarchy. Deadlines are missed and things don't get done, or they get done late and with too many compromises.

Resilience

Imagine a culture made up entirely of individuals with troubled backgrounds. Most of them have no family beyond others in this group itself. New members join at unpredictable intervals, and nobody can stay for long.

Brett Loftis leads such a culture. He is the CEO of Crossnore, one of the most successful orphanages in the United States. Crossnore was founded a century ago to help children find new beginnings. Success, to Brett, has many dimensions, among them malnutrition recovery, state exam proficiency, adoption placements, and college enrollment rates.

But ultimately, Brett's mission is to build a culture of resilience, both with respect to the often dreadful experiences these children have had by the time they arrive at Crossnore and as it relates to the challenges they will encounter as they embark on a life beyond the orphanage. Crossnore breaks generational cycles of poverty through new learned behaviors, rooted in the resilience to deal with a difficult past and face a future with challenges all its own.

Brett explains that there are "protective factors" in building resilience. Some of these are intrinsic, such as a sense of humor and the ability to delay gratification (remember the Marshmallow Test in Chapter Seven?), but many others are learned, among them planning for the future, building stable social relationships,[1] and developing empathy for the plight of others. It is the combination of these protective factors that allows for a future that is different from the past. As Brett told me, "Resilience, in the long run, is the ability to build something that did not exist before."

Resilient Cultures

There comes a point in many a sustainability transformation process in which it all starts to get hard. When senior leadership is on board and sustainability is widely viewed as an unavoidable mandate, the organization shifts into gear with concrete programs framed by appropriate financial, environmental, and social metrics. The time to make it all happen in real and substantial terms has arrived.

A critical cultural attribute at this stage is resilience, which we'll define as the ability of the organization to remain cohesive and composed under persistent internal or external stress and to effectively overcome resistance. Stress (which for our purposes you can think of as a persistent lack of control) and resistance can stem from a gap between the organization's aspirations and its actual performance (for example, during a product recall or the discovery of child labor in the supply chain) or can relate to the sustainability initiatives themselves. Members of a resilient culture rely on mutual trust and respect to constructively and transparently deal with conflict. They take responsibility for their actions, even (and particularly) when things go wrong, trusting the team to support them.

Resilience is reflected in everyday interactions. A culture with strong resilience elements displays trust, respect, and support—this is what sustains people under pressure, individually and collectively. There is an atmosphere of open feedback, but it is not all calm waters. Indeed, a culture with a strong resilience dimension is one that engages in constructive conflict. By contrast, a culture with poor resilience will display a lack of trust, a lack of respect, and a weak sense of belonging. People tend to avoid conflict and, when conflict arises, tend to move quickly into a blame game.

At low levels of resilience, a culture will act essentially as a collection of individuals. Think of it as social Brownian motion. Because people tend to lack mutual trust and respect, they not only blame one another or "them" in accounting, marketing, or manufacturing, as we saw in Chapter Ten. Here conflicts tend to may escalate quickly, and there may be an overriding sense that the members of this culture would readily trade their organization for another one.

A culture at a middle level of resilience is amicable, generally supportive of others, and able to sustain some pressure. There will be a basic level of trust and respect among members, but under pressure, members may point fingers rather than take responsibility. Members may try to manage conflicts constructively, but not always succeed. In a very challenging situation, trust is likely to break down, and members will question each other's abilities.

A highly resilient culture is tightly linked and mutually supportive, able to sustain tremendous pressure from the outside. There is very clear trust and respect among members of the culture, and conflict is dealt with in a constructive way. Members and teams freely discuss incidents and give feedback when tensions arise. They take responsibility for their actions, especially when things go wrong, knowing that the organization has their back.

What distinguishes highly resilient cultures is that they are much more comfortable with risk-taking and doing things in radically new ways. This not only makes them adaptive but also divides resilience into two types. Allow me to make an analogy borrowing from psychologist Jean Piaget. Piaget showed that to survive in an environment—to be resilient—individuals must adapt to external stimuli. The two mechanisms of adaptation are *assimilation* and *accommodation*.[2] The first of these, assimilation, is about processing new information with existing means. If you have never been in a hurricane, for example, you might use the same means to deal with it as you have successfully used in a rainstorm (seek shelter). In the case of the second, accommodation, the existing means are insufficient to deal with reality and must themselves be expanded, even if it is risky to do so. If the climate were to change, for instance, we might need new means to collectively address the issue or else be confined to assimilating to whatever environment we find ourselves in.

Resilience is similarly split. On the one hand, there is assimilating resilience, which is simply a graduation of the attribute displayed in low- and medium-resilience cultures. It is the moxie to bounce back from adversity, to overcome. It may be the type of resilience necessary to face a surprise move by a competitor or some other major adverse event. Highly resilient cultures prevail in the face of such challenges.

On the other hand, accommodating resilience is much more proactive and implies change in the culture itself. Accommodating resilience enables one to make difficult decisions in light of a challenging future (rather than to recover from a difficult past). Constant and iterative rather than episodic (as is inherent in assimilating resilience), it enables growth. Misleadingly, companies with accommodating resilience often appear lucky to have been dealt a better hand. Both types of resilience require courage, but accommodating resilience is more forward leaning: it anticipates—and in so doing enables transformative change. It's the one Brett Loftis has to get right to prepare Crossnore children for the future once they have made peace with the past. Why is accommodating resilience so important for cultures of purpose? Because although assimilating resilience (let's call it S-resilience) can help you catch up if you are behind, accommodating resilience (C-resilience) allows you to set the bar. The latter also lays the foundation for the openness I will describe in Chapter Twelve.

Here's an example of the transition from S- to C-resilience. If you drive from Montgomery, Alabama, to Tallahassee, Florida (or better yet, ride a motorcycle), at the halfway point you might find yourself in Enterprise, Alabama. As you come down Main Street, you will see the statue of a woman, thirteen feet tall, holding a pedestal with what on close inspection turns out to be a beetle. This beetle is the boll weevil, a Central American critter that migrated to the United States to become the most destructive cotton pest in history. It laid waste to southern farms in the first half of the twentieth century and has cost the domestic cotton industry over $13 billion. Why should there be a statue erected in its honor? Nowhere else in the world will you find a statue devoted to an insect pest. Indeed, the boll weevil appeared on the scene just as the Great Depression hit its stride, and many regarded it as a scourge of biblical proportions. But the citizens of Enterprise—once primarily cotton farmers—first dealt with the pest with classical S-resilience and then developed a different, more resilient view. The community transitioned to peanut farming, quickly and profitably, and remained committed to diversified farming practices even after cotton made a comeback. They so appreciated the future borne of the beetle's arrival that they erected the statue in its honor, dedicating it "in profound appreciation of the Boll Weevil and what it has done as the herald of prosperity." Call that C-resilience with a cherry on top.

A CEO of a company with S-resilience might say, "We made a mistake, and it's on me. I am sorry. And I guarantee that we'll emerge stronger from this crisis, and so will investors who stick with us. Bank on it." The corollary in a C-resilient culture would not wait for the mistake to arise: "If you buy into our approach, then invest in us. If not, don't invest in us." It's not that the latter culture is immune to crises; it's that it has chosen to create a framework of values to deal with crises before they arise, and finds stakeholders who buy into that approach.

It is rare for a public CEO to make the second kind of statement and dissuade any group of investors from buying his stock, along with abolishing earnings guidance and quarterly reports. But Unilever's CEO did just that. Next, let's look more closely at the culture that supports this kind of resilience.

Kees Takes a Stand for Shared Resilience

Unilever is a company that has actively been building its resilience—both types. Perhaps its most famous example comes in its groundbreaking marketing effort for Dove called Campaign for Real Beauty, which you will remember from Chapter Six. The Dove Campaign for Real Beauty was conceived in 2004 after market research indicated that only 4 percent of women consider themselves beautiful. The campaign showcased photographs of regular women (in place of professional models), taken by Annie Leibovitz. The decision to launch this campaign had been challenged, but was sustained by the resilience of people throughout the organization who believed in its power to transform the dialogue with the consumer. It was a defining moment for Unilever. It is also a great example of C-resilience: the organization did not wait for the market to voice dissatisfaction with body images; it asked the difficult questions and shaped the dialogue, even though doing so would clearly yield occasionally uncomfortable challenges.

Kees Kruythoff, Unilever's president of North America, had a front-row seat in this campaign. He tells us that the Dove campaign was no accident. And no single one-hit wonder. It was an outgrowth of the larger resilient nature the firm had developed and nurtured, even as it engaged in the complex and far-reaching art of global brand marketing.

Kees brings a bridge-minded view to his work for both the business and the environment. "Sustainability to me means drawing an arc from sustainable business—a business built to last—to a better life for consumers. The environment and equitable parts of growth are components of this arc."

And he notes that the founding of the company—by Lord Lever in 1930—even then had a mission of sustainability: "The biggest issue in Victorian England was hygiene, and Lord Lever made hygiene commonplace. Right from the beginning, Unilever was built to contribute to the biggest issues in society." That tradition continues today, he says. "The biggest issue currently in the world is sustainable living. So that's where we focus."

When Kees came to Unilever in 1993, he found a company engaged in sustainability issues—but often behind the scenes. "When I began my career at Unilever, we started sustainable fishing. It was clear that there weren't enough fish in the ocean; all the while we had fish fingers in Europe—it was part of our business," he says. "We did the right things, but we never linked it to our brands. When we had figured out sustainable fishing, you'd buy our fish fingers in Europe and not know that they were different. Only later did we learn to build how we do things into purpose-driven brands. That was a big step, and sometimes it's risky because we say what we stand for and need to deliver."

What has changed in the two decades since is Unilever's willingness to attack issues of sustainability in more open

191

and fluid public forums, to put itself "out there" and speak authentically about its aspirations. Sometimes this approach invites dissent and criticism, but when they arise, the organization is a participant in the dialogue rather than a spectator.

Unilever started the journey to establishing its own brand as a stamp of quality for sustainable living, which forges a global powerhouse but also exposes the company to the fates of each of its brands. A purpose-driven brand requires a complicated and labor-intensive strategy—one that puts the company in dialogue with a variety of constituencies and opens it to a variety of commentators, skeptics, and critics. Not all those conversations are comfortable or easy to manage. Resilience is a necessary constant companion.

C-resilience is crucial because resources are becoming less ubiquitous, consumer habits are changing, and demographics are evolving more rapidly than at any point in the past. Meanwhile, your products are becoming increasingly transparent, regardless of whether you want them to or not. We have entered the age of Caveat Venditor—Let the Seller Beware. The question is whether you will participate in and shape this transition. It will be uncomfortable—not all the feedback you get in a dialogue is positive, and some of it is unfit to print. But that's a cakewalk compared to not participating in the dialogue and reactively trying to find your way in an environment that has gotten away from you.

Achieving proactive resilience demands a willingness to engage in information gathering, even when doing so is inconvenient, whether in terms of content or of source.

Here is how participating feels in real time. When Kees worked for Unilever in South Africa, he stayed with a family to understand the local culture and customs. One day, he went to a grocery store in Soweto and saw that the price for their margarine was wrong. He called the office and said, "What's going on? The price should be 4.99—why is it 5.25?" Kees smiles, adding: "They had a shock. They said: *Why are you there?* Let alone checking prices." But Kees was doing more than checking the price; he was demonstrating the need for information to flow back to the company. He was standing shoulder to shoulder with his customers and listening. "If you're in consumer goods, you can only succeed if you're really close to society. You need to be right alongside them, live where they live, shop where they shop, and most importantly listen to them along the way. You can't do that from headquarters."

This transparency, in turn, gives rise to C-resilience by forcing the organization to get ahead of potential issues rather than wait for their ramifications to become clear. And that makes it much easier to deal with even the most difficult of corporate actions: acknowledging and fixing an error. Here's how Kees explains the Unilever policy toward recalls—it is a process with C-resilience running through it, although many recalls are exercises in S-resilience.

"When we had recalls in the business, it was always an easy trade-off; in fact there was no trade-off. If there is something wrong, we never compromise. Never. We already made the real decision long before the actual event, so this is simply a logical step," Kees says, succinctly articulating proactive resilience. "If we are in doubt, we fully recall it. We always will. Of course, there is an immediate cost effect in it. But it's just never a discussion." This happened recently in Brazil, he says, when an audit revealed a packaging issue that could lead consumers to misunderstand which container held a beverage and which one cleaning fluid. "Immediately we recalled the whole lot even beyond the affected product so that consumers were not confused. These are things which are absolutely nonnegotiable." Note how C-resilience outpaces S-resilience (which would have taken a more statistical approach in reacting to a product problem).

What I noticed in my conversations with Kees was his pride in working for a company that behaves this way. In saying "We always will," Kees demonstrates his strong sense of belonging. This sense is a hallmark of cultures that sustain themselves for a long time. The Romani, for instance, have different words for *woman/man* or *girl/boy* depending on whether others are themselves Romani, effectively bifurcating all people into insiders and outsiders. Given that gypsies have been around as a distinct culture for many thousands of years, it's worth taking note. We should be mindful, however, that when a culture becomes too tribal, C-resilience decreases and the first casualty is openness, the topic of the next chapter.

Some companies agonize about recalls. Unilever does not. Because they agonized about the bigger values long before, they are able to face any recall with clarity. But that does not mean the company never gets caught on the back foot.

Consider the story of Unilever and its purchase of Ben & Jerry's Ice Cream.

194

Ben & Jerry's was founded by two childhood friends, Ben Cohen and Jerry Greenfield, in Burlington, Vermont, in 1978. In addition to churning out popular flavors like Chunky Monkey and Chocolate Chip Cookie Dough, the company was well known for its progressive activism. In its early days, it had a wage-cap policy which ensured that no employee's rate of pay would exceed five times that of entry-level employees. It established a nonprofit called "1% for Peace," which set a goal to redirect 1 percent of the national defense budget to fund peace-promoting activities and projects. It made the leap to ecofriendly paperboard in its packaging.

Then it was purchased by Unilever.

Some wondered if the corporate giant would quash the ice cream company's activist voice. But the opposite was true. Unilever, demonstrating its corporate capacity for resilience in the face of challenges (now coming from inside the company), embraced Ben & Jerry's and every difficult discussion that came with the brand.

On April Fool's Day in 2009, Ben & Jerry's announced that it was behind the marketing campaign for CyClone Dairy, a fictional company selling milk only from cloned cows. The joke was a dig at the use of GMO materials by food producers and part of Ben & Jerry's demand for mandatory labeling of GMO foods. Not exactly what the parent company had on its policy books, but Unilever engaged in (rather than quashed) the debate with its subsidiary. Says Kees: "These challenges of brands within a portfolio developing different interpretations of how to pursue our purpose are here to stay. We are learning how to be part of the dialogue rather than shy away from it."

Part of being ready rather than shying away from challenges is having invited dissenters along the way, as Unilever did in setting up an independent Ben & Jerry's board at the time of the acquisition. Not many companies would contemplate such a construct, but Unilever did it.

Kees recalls a senior executive seminar in which twenty-five Unilever executives were gathered to forge a strategy for emerging markets: "We invited a powerful analyst for consumer goods, who was openly critical of Unilever's performance." Here was somebody clearly willing—indeed eager—to shake up the status quo with his criticism. But by making him part of the dialogue, Unilever afforded itself the opportunity to participate and to shape the dialogue rather than react to it.

The seminar was also, Kees realized later, a gathering of the future leaders of Unilever. "Many of the participants of that seminar are now in the Unilever executive team. So this was literally the future leaders dealing with tough questions and opposition," he says.

This is the attitude—the resilience—that Unilever CEO Paul Polman drew on when he told the bottom-line fixated analysts to back off. "We want the quality of our investors to reflect the quality of our stock, and it does. That's why the volatility of our stock has decreased so much," Kees reflects. "We know that because we do the right thing for consumers, for shoppers, for society, together with our suppliers and together with our customers and investors, the rest will work out. Even when things are tough, even when we make mistakes, it will work out as long as we go after the right thing, and it will create more value for all our shareholders."

And C-resilience will lead them forward.

■ ■ ■

Surprise, criticism, conflict, failure. All of these can become opportunities in a resilient culture. Kees's experience shows that, first, a resilient culture has mechanisms to deal with constructive feedback, even if painful. Issuing comprehensive product recalls in response to customer confusion is an example of this. Second, resilience means being cognizant of future challenges and willing to take risks to head them off (C-resilience). Think back to Unilever's willingness to endow Ben & Jerry's with its own board, knowing that the two companies would disagree at times. Third, and most important, resilience is built on a sense of belonging and trust. Trust that the culture as a whole is eager to do the right thing and that the actions of individuals reflect this aspiration. It is this trust that enabled Unilever to open its doors to invite in its critics, as it did in Kees's leadership meeting.

Understanding the Culture: Markers for the Attribute of Resilience

Resilience can seem like a daunting cultural attribute to cultivate. And it does take courage. But it can be easier than you think. In psychology, there is the concept of *emergent norm theory*, which basically holds that crowd behavior emerges spontaneously after people have milled about for a while, allowing leaders to emerge. Similarly, cultures form around

197

the behaviors your leaders model. The key behavior found in a resilient culture is trust. Together, trust and purpose make for a very powerful combination that enables a tightly linked, mutually supportive culture.

The objective of a resilient culture is not to eliminate failure. It's to succeed by failing fast, failing cheap, and failing often. And to learn all along the way. Resilient cultures don't just celebrate successes; they acknowledge, discuss, even memorialize their failures. The bounce-back is part of what makes the company what it is. This is a group that cheers the candid, the difficult, and the challenging. It is a culture willing to do the hard work for a big goal. It is a group unafraid to try, fail, and try again. The following questions are crafted to uncover the degree to which a culture displays resilience.

What to Look For	How to Look for It
People at all levels of the culture have strong bonds built on trust.	What has been your favorite failure? How did you share it with others?
	When have you experienced the sense of belonging to this company most forcefully?
Conflict is dealt with openly and constructively.	When have leaders of the company been candidly challenged by others?
	What causes conflict to simmer here?
External pressures are viewed as constructive forces. (Hi there, boll weevil.)	How do you engage with your clients and consumers?
	How have you seen teams in this organization behave when they are under pressure? What was the pressure, and what behavior did you observe?

What to Look For	How to Look for It
The culture shares a perspective on the right thing to do and the need to stand up for it.	When have you agonized about something that seemed the right thing to do? What happened? When have you decided to lead the market on a controversial issue rather than follow?
The culture has learned to pivot from S- to C-resilience.	Where has your company led in establishing what "good" looks like? How difficult was it? When do you share your nonfinancial performance metrics, and how do you decide to share nonregulated information in general?
The culture comprehensively defines its stakeholders and seeks input from all of them.	How do you engage with external stakeholders and involve them in your dialogue? Who are they? Who is most critical of your product, and why?
Although values are firm, the modus operandi is met with irreverence.	What will always be true about this company? What did you think would always be true that has turned out not to be? What changed?
The culture learns, and uses the new information to iterate its approach.	How have you seen this organization evolve as a result of external input and open debate? What can this company be most proud to have learned?

Red Flags: The most common deterrent of resilience is a bureaucracy. This one is not always obvious on first glance. Bureaucratic cultures rely on highly regimented ways of working and limited channels of communication both internally and with the world outside. As a result, the quantity and quality of information that reaches and is digested by the organization are greatly reduced. Revealing the interconnectedness of the three cultural attributes, the telltale signs of a bureaucracy are low openness and low energy. It is slow to respond to critical needs and to see change, and it rejects quick action or outside opinions about what needs to be done. As a result, such cultures are often preoccupied with internal processes.

Openness

When Ward Cunningham came of age as a computer programmer, the prevailing logic was that to create greatness in programming, you should lock yourself in a room and fully define your destination before starting to write code. And if that did not get you to the right place, lock yourself in the room longer.

But Ward's life was more than computers; he was also an avid reader. He read broadly and deeply the works of linguists, evolutionary biologists, architects, and philosophers. This reading bled into his view of programming. Everything Ward had learned about cultures and evolution and design suggested that there was a better, more iterative way to foster emergent design—a way that exploits distributed and unconscious knowledge.

So when Ward created the code infrastructure for the world's first wiki in the early 1990s, he traded away control for trust in revolutionizing the way people work together and

200

learn in groups. What resulted were systems that allowed for the iterative evolution of knowledge, placing far more value on the ease of correcting mistakes than on the difficulty of making them. Ward reflects: "From the very beginning of the wiki, people routinely startled themselves by what they could achieve together."

I took away three key points from my conversation about openness with Ward. First, meet the status quo with both courtesy and irreverence. Which approach turns out to be appropriate will become clear in time. Second, as already noted, maximize the ease of correcting mistakes rather than the difficulty of making them. The best way to get the right answer on the Internet is not to ask a question, Ward told me, but "to post the wrong answer." And finally, be receptive to where ideas from unexpected sources lead you: your most interesting path forward may not be the one you thought you'd find yourself on.

Open Cultures

One of my clients grappling with the challenges of opening up his organization once told me, "I realized that I could no longer complain about how stodgy our culture is, because I have been here long enough, have become senior enough, to *be* the culture." It reminded me of a sign on the side of the road. It read, "You are not stuck in traffic. You *are* traffic."

Openness is about getting unstuck. This cultural attribute describes the degree to which the people inside your organization are connected to and engaged with each other and the outside world. It implies a heightened state of external awareness—the ability to be receptive to external input and not only be stimulated by it but also willing to adapt as a result of it. Open cultures proactively draw in information and adapt to the new information they receive.

When we have helped our clients assess their culture, we have often found that openness is the most elusive attribute. It can be difficult to behave openly, to "open up." It's scary to muster the nerve to ask the difficult questions, scarier to know that anybody around you can ask them at any time.

In a culture of openness, critical thinking and debate are encouraged. People challenge themselves by seeking new information, best practices, and outside participants to question current thinking. Innovation jams and skip-level meetings, for example, are tools for open cultures.

Openness is a critical part of a culture of purpose because it helps ensure that relevant themes and influences are identified and acted on. It is not unusual for a sustainability vision to lack granularity—particularly after an initial phase of the sustainability team's work. In order to move through that fog and define a clear path forward, people throughout the organization must individually and collectively be able to listen to and synthesize the views of a broad spectrum of stakeholders. This is the process that allows leaders to move beyond the superficial level of sustainability leadership and push on to more robust and resonant efforts.

As we will see in Chapter Thirteen, openness certainly matters in the early stages of the journey to engage with the broader organization and the outside world, but it becomes increasingly crucial thereafter, when discrete and targeted programs are evolving into sustainability efforts that encompass every aspect of operations and long-term strategy.

At a glance, it's possible to discern the openness (or lack thereof) of an organization. Cultures exhibiting a low level of this attribute are closed to ideas and to people considered outsiders. A moderate degree of openness brings receptivity to new input and acceptance of new data, but cultures at this level are not always proactive when it comes to seeking outside perspectives. In organizations operating at the highest levels of openness, the culture is very well connected, both inside and outside the company. The trick is to be nimble yet hold on to "that thing" which defines your culture.

Alberto Exposes Shared Openness

What does openness look like? It's a concept that seems familiar to us on its face, yet the expression of openness in a culture of purpose is multifaceted. Alberto Weisser spent fourteen years leading the agribusiness giant Bunge. During his tenure, he fostered openness across the company in a variety of contexts, demonstrating both its complexity and its power for driving sustainable change and a culture of purpose.

Alberto moved through his executive career with a passion for trust and transparency. He saw it not just as a business strategy but as a guiding principle for his actions both in and outside the corporate structure. But his career leading up to Bunge had left him dissatisfied.

"I had seen very cynical environments and wanted an open one," he says. In his previous leadership roles, he participated in efforts to introduce improvements to the corporate culture, vision, and mission. But in his mind, they fell short.

At its core, openness is about how you deal with people, he says. "Openness means that you speak up if you see something is off; you have to say it. You can't hide information, and you have to be very honest and fess up to problems. And that's true whether I have a product issue or when somebody wants to know why he was not promoted. I have to be honest about it, even if it hurts."

Implicit in the willingness to endure the pains of openness was Alberto's realization that the opposite of openness did not yield greater comfort. He shared that when he was a boy, he lied to his mother ("I did not break that vase!") and felt terrible about it. That feeling stayed with him when he saw a business he worked in early in his career do "monkey deals" that smacked of corrupt practices; he realized that business could be conducted cleanly, openly—and ultimately leave everybody feeling better and proud. Pain be damned.

That means scaling up from individual interactions, guiding not just one-on-one encounters but the way a culture interacts internally and with the rest of the planet.

It began with the engagement of outsiders. Alberto became a pioneer for Bunge in reaching out to external stakeholders on the topic of sustainability. Often the activities took different names—as everywhere, the word *sustainable* in Bunge's home country of Brazil has been overused and has lost impact in the wider business conversation.

204

His earliest challenges revolved around Bunge's inertia in launching sustainability efforts. He turned to openness, reaching outside the walls of his firm to start the process.

He began by meeting with Brazilian officials—everyone from the president to the office of Brazil's top environmental agency. "I had a meeting with the head of the environmental agency of Brazil, and the minister didn't want to receive me, but I was received by the secretary, the number two." The fact that Alberto saw him against the advice of many around him, who considered this official too fundamentalist and aggressive, reveals another facet of openness: the unwillingness to be constrained by either hierarchy or ideology.

Alberto spent hours with the secretary and his team. Starting with ten people in the room that day, Bunge helped launch a program that became famous, the Soy Moratorium. This is a cross-sector initiative spanning the government, Greenpeace, and Bunge's entire industry. Alberto says, "We discovered that soy had an indirect impact on deforestation because of the land reselling effect. Working with the government and the whole industry, we were able to make sure that all of the industry would not buy any more soybeans from newly deforested land." Along the way, Bunge had the openness to partner not only with government and NGOs but also with its competitors Cargill, ADM, and Dreyfus. Indeed, the notion of co-opetition is central to highly open cultures.

This story demonstrates the openness not only to ask the right questions and follow the answers but also to engage with regulators, critics, and competitors to bring about real solutions. It was the combination of the main industry players,

205

partnered with Greenpeace and the government dedicated to enforcement through satellite mapping, that allowed the project to reduce deforesting, Alberto says. Not only was the environmental impact significant, but Alberto credited the initiative with changing the mind-set in his industry. It also changed the Brazilian government, which recognized the power of partnering with corporate players.

And perhaps most intimately, it changed Bunge inside. Quite suddenly, Alberto's team started to look at sustainability and the environment as something positive. Alberto says, "The moratorium was never meant to be permanent. It was a shock to the system in a way—a way to change perceptions and conversations, and start a collaborative process to a longer-term solution. And it has really worked. Under the umbrella of citizenship, sustainability became a value of Bunge. The employees demanded it. They wanted Bunge to state that we are here to positively impact the communities we operate in."

Indeed, Alberto was aware that in order to shape culture, he had to make openness an attribute of life at Bunge, not just a facet of his personal style. That was difficult, because in the beginning, Alberto says, "I faced hostility everywhere. We saw ourselves solely tasked with making money—at the expense of everything." Alberto became known as "the green guy" (not a compliment, he notes), and many were simply confused about what he was after. So when Alberto, convinced that partnering with others would accelerate Bunge's progress, built an alliance with Conservation International, he personally led the charge together with his head of communications and PR. "At first, I had to do it myself," he says.

Alberto designed the effort to spread through the organization as it gained momentum. It was built around a simple idea. The Brazilian environmental laws are very good, but not well enforced, he says. They stipulate that each farmer needs to leave a certain amount of virgin land. But because it doesn't make sense to have little parcels of virgin land on each individual farm, Conservation International came up with the concept of building corridors—connecting the parcels. "So we needed to convince dozens of farmers in a given area to combine these islands into a corridor," Alberto says.

Many of the farmers had to be convinced and helped to go along with the plan, but in the end, they did. Alberto and Conservation International assisted the farmers in creating a large corridor where the fauna and flora could develop. Eventually (to the surprise of the employees and Alberto himself), the farmers agreed and in fact liked the idea. Alberto says: "It spread like a virus. People said, 'Wait a minute: the farmers are in agreement with it!'"

The echo of this success rippled through Bunge, as employees increasingly voiced their desire to collaborate with different communities. Alberto could not have been happier. He approved new policies that allowed employees to devote a portion of their work hours to do volunteer community work. This, in turn, exposed the entire company to new influences from farmers, from community organizers, and of course from Conservation International. From a tactical perspective, Alberto was able to drive meaningful and lasting change in the Brazilian farmlands. Strategically, however, he was after bigger game: he was opening up the culture of Bunge.

Alberto did not just rely on those with whom he could personally engage for advice and input. Throughout his efforts, he extended his open approach to embrace new ideas—even from individuals he may not have had the opportunity to meet. He engaged continually in the search for best practices, whether by conversing with an airline seatmate or reading a book. In fact, throughout our conversation, Alberto was inquisitive about the arc of the story I was crafting and the lessons underpinning it. He is informed by his passion for reading history and the biographies of great world leaders, quoting John Boyd, Martin Van Creveld, and Ulysses S. Grant.

Perhaps one of the most challenging expressions of openness comes when Alberto finds himself face-to-face with uncomfortable information. Moving into a more sustainable process nearly always requires confronting, discussing, and exposing processes that have been taken for granted. Challenging established practices is rarely popular. Yet the willingness to look for and synthesize uncomfortable information is the most telling expression of openness.

Openly confronting a long-held practice is hard on everyone. Alberto gave an example: "I publicly say that what we are doing in Kansas on the High Plains and Ogallala Aquifers is wrong. And the employees hear this and ask me, 'Yes, but what about the farmer?'" Alberto pauses as he distills his message to its elemental core: "It is *wrong*. The farmer should be producing something else, not grain, because grain consumes too much water. Other crops could grow on that land. But we have to be honest with each other, and the truth has to be heard."

Because Alberto was pursuing openness as a cultural attribute—as a fundamental trait of Bunge's DNA—he did not shy away from carrying controversial issues to an even wider audience.

Take, for example, the topic of obesity. It's a touchy subject for a food supplier. Alberto joined the board of Pepsi in part to bring more exposure and debate of health and environmental issues to the corporate conversation.

Alberto acknowledges that his company is challenging its suppliers and customers, the farmers. But being open does not mean you have all the answers. It does mean that you are honest when you don't. For example, "When it comes to meat, we haven't yet figured out how to do it," Alberto says. And by being open himself, he makes it possible for others within Bunge to do the same.

"In a culture of openness, people have to speak up," Alberto says. "So I make sure there is no witch hunt. Making a mistake does not mean punishment—not so for hiding one. Instead, we'll get it out in the open and say, 'OK, that was not right.' People need to be comfortable about speaking up and saying something." As CEO, Alberto was aware that the authority of his title could serve to shield against divergent views of others. Indeed, it has long been known that obedience to authority figures can be more powerful than conscience. A famous example of this is the Milgram experiment, in which volunteers, prodded by an authoritative experimental scientist at Yale University, were brought to administer what they thought were increasingly powerful electric shocks to another person.[1]

Preemptively banishing the resulting confirmation bias that can sneak into the executive suite, Alberto points out that "I encourage discussions. Is meat something bad for the world? Because to consume one pound of meat you need five pounds of grain. Grain needs water. So are we creating a mess in the world? Some people say, 'Yes, but our biggest customer is the meat industry.'" Alberto arches his brows: "So what?! We could change our business to something else. I encourage people—our scientists—to study whether palm oil is really bad!" He returns to his initial question: "Are we doing something wrong? We need people to look for things that are wrong as part of our integrity." It is the same mind-set that allows Bunge also to see what could be better, not just to do less of some kinds of business but to create and grow new ones that are matched to the needs of the twenty-first century.

One reason he continued to talk about these issues is that Alberto is able to see the impact of openness across the spectrum of his experience. From the vantage point of a fourteen-year CEO, he could see the cultural impact of openness. Recruits to the company list sustainability and Bunge's transparency as a key reason they chose Bunge as an employer. Alberto knew that existing employees are inspired by that same openness and strike out to find new ways for Bunge to prosper.

Alberto likes to brag about the activity that erupted in his company at the intersection of openness and entrepreneurial thinking. When he started, Bunge was so unused to sustainability efforts, he had to personally lead and fund the initial programs. Over the course of his tenure, his model of openness and inquiry led to efforts all over the company—some of which he didn't learn about until after the fact.

"It's the spirit of entrepreneurship. What I tell people is to just do it, but live the values. You cannot compromise the values. Let the good ideas come up. It took me a while to understand it, but great things happened early on when an idea I might have thought was mine was presented to me by my employees, and then saying, wow, that's a great idea. They will implement that idea with a completely different energy if it is theirs." He adds, "And now, often the very best ideas—which I could never have thought of—are fully functioning initiatives by the time I hear about them." True, these initiatives were often individually small, but collectively they shaped the path of Bunge as employees used openness to tap into their entrepreneurial DNA.

Moving from CEO to chairman at Bunge, Alberto continued to press his vision for openness and discussion as a way to change the world for the better—wherever the dialogue leads.

When I asked him if this pursuit extends into his personal life, he nodded. "It's problematic to eat ice cream, for example," he says. "My wife hates me for saying it, but come on: it's sugar and fat." Looking down, he adds with a smile: "But of course I eat ice cream sometimes. And I am overweight, so I am part of the problem." Clearly, the openness that is core to the culture Alberto created applies equally to himself.

■ ■ ■

Cultures of purpose are borne out of focused actions. That means, first, insisting on mutual learning between the

211

core and the frontier of an organization. So when Alberto defines openness as "speaking up when you see something is off," he is not describing the duty of a CEO, but the privilege of any employee in an open culture. Second, open cultures speak honestly about mistakes and missteps; they admit what they don't know. As we saw at Bunge, that means no witch hunt or blaming. It also means questioning the fundamental underpinnings of the business model, trusting that a culture capable of finding fault with the modus operandi of its past will also be capable of charting a better path into the future. When confronted with information that might seem counter to prevailing business logic, Alberto's position was, "So what?! We could change our business to something else." Third, as Chapter Eleven foreshadowed with C-resilience, openness means inviting external critics, competitors, and detractors inside. Bunge's partnership with NGOs and competitors for the Soy Moratorium showcased this dimension of openness.

Understanding the Culture: Markers for the Attribute of Openness

As a leader, you have countless opportunities to open up your own organization, some when you are on stage in front of everybody, others as you are riding the elevator with an intern. You should seize as many of them as you possibly can because an open culture is smarter and ultimately more sustainable. It knows more about its competitive environment and will react more nimbly, whether iteratively or fundamentally.

Openness is an attribute that permeates every part of a culture. It shows up in the way managers interact with their direct reports, the way teams interact with each other, the way the company interacts with the outside world—customers, vendors, regulators, all. Openness allows for debate, experimentation, failure, and whistleblowing. It also creates an environment of trust and appreciation for competing ideologies. Look for the feedback opportunities, the conversation platforms, the ways discussion can happen. These are the signs that you're looking at an open culture.

The following questions are devised to expose how open a culture is.

What to Look For	How to Look for It
The organization maximizes the ease of correcting mistakes rather than the difficulty of making them.	Are there witch hunts? Can you think about a time that a mistake was celebrated? How does this organization learn from mistakes? Can you give me a recent specific example and tell me about the mechanisms in place to accelerate learning?
People throughout the organization are highly connected with each other and externally.	How do people tap into the organization and beyond to create feedback loops for their teams? What's the most insightful lesson that came from the outside? How did it get in?
Trust and transparency beat cynicism and hierarchy.	Why is there a separate elevator to the executive floor? Do you have "black teams"[2] or another mechanism to discuss and learn from mistakes?
People throughout the organization feel compelled to speak up and act.	Were you ever surprised to find your point of view challenged in a venue you thought inappropriate? How do you reinforce the ability of people to contribute their thoughts to a larger dialogue? Specifically what do you do?

What to Look For	How to Look for It
Difficult messages or shocks to the system are not avoided.	What topics are sacred cows around here? Is feedback given routinely and omnidirectionally? What was the most shaping feedback you have received?
Competitors and critics are brought inside.	Have you had whistleblowers? What's the greatest public challenge for the organization, and how are you dealing with it?
The organization is honest about what it does not know and is keen to learn from any informed source.	When have you admitted internally or externally that you didn't know how to go about doing something? Who was the most surprising contributor you invited into the process of crafting a solution?
Ownership of ideas is secondary to their quality, and the best ideas are copied shamelessly.	What ideas can this organization be most proud to have stolen from others? How many of this company's great ideas originate with management as opposed to the shop floor?

Red Flags: The greatest challenge to openness is a tribal culture, which exacerbates low openness with a lack of balance. Balance, as a cultural attribute, describes the degree to which organizations not only include a diversity of perspectives, skills, and styles but also express, recognize, and leverage the resulting differences. And the less a culture is balanced, the more openness will suffer. If companies could get moldy, this would be how.

PART 4

Taking Action

Everything up to now has been about the building blocks of a culture of purpose—the competencies, traits, and attributes at its core. It's a lot of stuff. But it need not be overwhelming, because there is a clear sequence to building such a culture.

That's good news for two reasons. First, having a playbook focuses leaders on a subset of these building blocks at any one point in the transformation of their organization. Second, it yields a clear starting point.

The final chapter of this book structures competencies, traits, and attributes into an actionable plan. I will describe the three-phase process that synthesizes these concepts and show how they work together toward a culture of purpose.

The Sequence of Building a Culture of Purpose

Since its founding in 2008, Egon Zehnder's Sustainability Practice has executed hundreds of mandates matching strategy and talent. The model described in this chapter distills these experiences, dividing the rise of a culture of purpose into three phases.[1] Each phase calls for a specific set of building blocks and is separated from the next by demarcation points that will help you determine where you are. The figure on the next page summarizes the three phases and connects each to the leadership competencies, individual traits, and cultural attribute that characterize them.

The Starting Point

The Dunning-Kruger effect is a phenomenon in human psychology that is exhibited by people who confidently but mistakenly rate their ability at a given task much higher than average.[2] It's the cognitive bias of not knowing what one doesn't

The Sequence of Building a Culture of Purpose with Sustainability

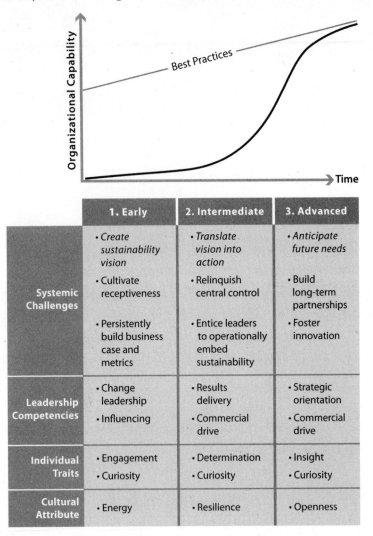

	1. Early	2. Intermediate	3. Advanced
Systemic Challenges	• *Create sustainability vision* • Cultivate receptiveness • Persistently build business case and metrics	• *Translate vision into action* • Relinquish central control • Entice leaders to operationally embed sustainability	• *Anticipate future needs* • Build long-term partnerships • Foster innovation
Leadership Competencies	• Change leadership • Influencing	• Results delivery • Commercial drive	• Strategic orientation • Commercial drive
Individual Traits	• Engagement • Curiosity	• Determination • Curiosity	• Insight • Curiosity
Cultural Attribute	• Energy	• Resilience	• Openness

know, and wrongly assuming that one knows quite a bit. An equivalent effect is in play in organizations that are at the starting point of the sustainability journey toward a culture of purpose. The culture is *unconsciously reactive* to issues of sustainability. What I mean by that is that the organization is largely unaware of what sustainability means in the context of its business and will grapple with the issue only tactically, in response to an event or an imminent need.

Leadership tends to view sustainability as a nonissue or perhaps as an annoying but necessary regulatory constraint. Government rules may be part of the company process, but there are no internal business metrics used to measure sustainable practices. They're not considered important or pressing, and in the vernacular of the company are simply data.

Phase One: The Early Stage

In Phase One, information is assembled from data as cultures gradually become conscious of their reactive stance with respect to sustainability. They initially do not know, in other words, what sustainability means for them and view it principally as a way of overcoming challenges to the business. A company in need of a natural resource to create its product might begin to think actively about the impact of water shortages or defor-estation on its business model. The sustainability theme comes to them in the form of a business problem. During this phase, organizations will engage with the topic in a substantive way when prompted—perhaps in response to new regulation or to the vocal protests of visible activist groups.

From a sustainability perspective, the challenge during this phase is to create a sustainability vision—one that aligns with the purpose of the company. From a cultural perspective, the challenge is to jolt the organization with the energy it needs to become aware of its passive stance, to become *conscious of its reactivity*. In the context of the competencies of your leadership—the building blocks you can control directly and with short-term impact—success in this phase requires change leadership and the ability to influence others.

Key Leadership Competencies

Change Leadership

The first step in any substantive transformation is to prepare for change. Change leadership is a particular kind of leadership—one that must acknowledge the turmoil it necessarily creates. As you saw in Chapter One with Frank O'Brien-Bernini, the point at which ideas mature into action is often the first real movement of a transformation.

Influencing

For change to scale, it must move from the heads of a few into the collective consciousness. You can order your direct reports to follow your lead, but to bring the rest of the organization (and sometimes beyond) with you, you will need to influence others. Like change leadership, this is a competency—one that can be learned and taught and practiced. Chapter Two, featuring Pascal Mittermaier, provides a road map for his influencing approach.

■ ■ ■

Those are the key competencies for the most effective leaders in navigating Phase One. But leaders, by definition, need others. During Phase One, the key trait of the people throughout the organization, and in particular the key trait of new people being hired in and evolving the culture, is engagement. Keep in mind that traits are fundamental to who a person is; they are part of one's construct rather than learned.

Key Individual Trait

Engagement

As the organization starts on its journey, people who can engage others and are themselves engaged by the purpose of the culture are crucial multipliers all the way out to the frontiers of the company. If sustainability is a (good) virus, people with engagement are its vector. Perhaps the deer-hunting accountant driving a pickup seems indifferent to recycling. But he's the one who can convince twenty coworkers to show up on a Saturday to pick up trash at a playground. He is an individual with a clear need for engagement in his own life, and he's the type who can spread that sense of urgency to others. In Chapter Six, you saw the career trajectory of John Replogle and learned how his own inner need for engagement led him to make decisions that brought him closer and closer to a culture of purpose. And along the way, he spread that inner drive to those around him through his enthusiasm, his work ethic, and his unwillingness to live an unengaged life.

Key Cultural Attribute

Energy

Finally, the culture is the glue holding your people together. And the cultural attribute necessary to succeed in Phase One is energy.

When a fox chases a rabbit, the rabbit usually gets away. Why? The rabbit is not faster. He's not smarter. But he is running for his life, whereas the fox is merely running for dinner. Dinner is nice, but getting Phase One right means making it about life. When you are the rabbit, you have plenty of energy.

For a primer on finding and cultivating energy, flip back to Chapter Ten and the story of Bob Kidder, who shares with us three vignettes from his career, each of which provides a perspective on infusing organizations with energy. Without an energized culture, nothing will happen.

Cultural Pitfall

Phase One has its unique set of challenges, the most prominent of which you can think of as the debating society I described at the end of Chapter Ten. As a leader, you count on what you hope is an energetic culture of engaged people, but you might instead find that a lot of time and effort is consumed in debate. This is a dysfunctional mode that must be dealt with early if the transformation is to progress to Phase Two.

How do you know if the culture is stuck in the rut of a debating society? The arguments don't stop. Decisions, therefore, are put off. This results in missed deadlines and frequent failure to get things done, or things get done late and over budget. If the only agreement you seem to be hearing is that "there's more to be said, and others don't understand the issues," you might be mired in a debating society. The culture needs to be energized to move forward, accepting trade-offs and keeping debates to their time and place. As you saw with Bob Kidder, alignment of purpose, accountability, and risk-taking are effective tools for getting unstuck.

Phase Two: The Intermediate Phase

I'll call this the middle ground. Just as Phase One created information where previously there were data, Phase Two advances information to knowledge. You're looking for ways to embed sustainability practices in everyday operations. That means relinquishing central control and increasingly pushing autonomy to the frontier of the organization.

From a sustainability perspective, Phase Two must succeed in translating the vision of Phase One into action. That's not a trivial thing, and you can expect to encounter hurdles as the never-done-ness of what's ahead of you becomes apparent. For this reason, from a cultural perspective, this phase requires the resilience of the organization to overcome difficulties and stay true to its path. And as you have seen, resilience has a forward-leaning dimension, which allows the organization to become *consciously proactive*. It slowly begins to deal with sustainability as a way of creating business for challenges rather than just overcoming challenges to business. The required leadership competencies in this phase show a bias for action. They are commercial drive and results delivery.

Key Leadership Competencies

Commercial Drive

Companies, at least good ones, make money. This skill applied to a sustainability transformation marries the goals of sustainability and profitability. They are intertwined, rather than traveling on separate tracks in the organization. For a blueprint, flip back to Chapter Four and the work of Curtis Ravenel at Bloomberg. It was his commercial drive that helped his company create products in the field of sustainability that are profitable to both Bloomberg and its clients.

Results Delivery

This is the competency that takes the debate and kicks it into action. At this phase in the transformation, the time comes to focus on goals and move. As you saw with Andy Ruben at Walmart in Chapter Five, it requires leaders who are oriented toward action and motivated by metrics.

Key Individual Trait

Determination

When it comes to individual traits, as a leader, you are looking to tap the most determined. Determination is often evident in an individual at an early age.

These are the people who as children were undaunted—completing thousand-piece jigsaw puzzles, getting back on the skateboard with bruised shins. They stayed focused and met the challenges head-on. These determined individuals are crucial to Phase Two, because often this is where high-minded dreaming meets the cold reality of hard work. Phase Two can be a long and brutal period in which some things go well and other efforts spiral and crash. Determined people will see you through. For a close-up view of determination at work, look back at Chapter Seven for the story of Peter Bakker. His willingness to persevere through the challenging, action-oriented period of change is what helped his company deliver.

Key Cultural Attribute

Resilience

Being unconscious of the challenges ahead makes for a pretty comfortable state of affairs. But when an organization transitions from *unconscious* to *conscious* and from *reactive* to *proactive* on sustainability, there are growing pains and pushback. For this reason, sustainability transformation at this phase requires a good measure of resilience. It is time to hold fast and allow for failure, knowing that early missteps clarify the way forward. For a picture of a resilient culture, look back at Chapter Eleven and the experience of Kees Kruythoff of Unilever. Adapting to the new landscape both reactively and proactively is the privilege of resilient cultures.

Cultural Pitfall

The dysfunctional mode at this stage of transformation is one of bureaucracy. As you will recall from the last paragraphs of Chapter Eleven, what I mean by that is the highly regimented ways of working that can stifle a culture. Communication may be constrained by hierarchy and rules. This limits the quantity and quality of information that gets shared, which in turn makes resilience difficult to come by.

What does a bureaucracy look like? You'll see a culture that is likely to reject action or outside opinions on what needs to be done. This is a culture that has become too internally focused. It is too concerned with how it is functioning to adapt to the complexity and demands of Phase Two. The Unilever example shows that willful exposure to foreign voices is an effective way of overcoming this challenge.

Phase Three: The Advanced Phase

In the advanced phase of this transformation, sustainability and purpose truly merge. And as you already know, it's not about being nice to trees or bringing back the dodo. It's a state in which an organization both does well and does good in its present day without compromising its purpose for the future. In Phase Three, knowledge of issues becomes insight and ultimately foresight.

From a sustainability perspective, Phase Three enables an organization to anticipate future needs. Culturally, that implies openness to considering a wide spectrum of inputs as the organization operationalizes and becomes *unconsciously proactive* about the tactical elements of sustainability and can thus devote more bandwidth to far-out issues. This is a phase in which leaders will seek to build long-term partnerships. They will also look for ways to foster innovation, secure in the realization that the best ideas may be yet to come. Commercial drive continues as a vital competency from Phase Two, but is now augmented by strategic orientation.

Key Leadership Competency

Strategic Orientation

Thinking strategically means expanding perspectives through time, both up and down the value chain from the point of harvest to the point of purchase and across industries. Jochen Zeitz at PUMA showed this expanded view in Chapter Five when he established the environmental P&L and scaled impact across the global Kering portfolio. Accompanying strategic orientation is commercial drive, which continues as a differentiating competency from the second to the third phase, as expressed by the question Jochen Zeitz posed: "If Earth were a business, what would it charge us to use its resources?"

Key Individual Traits

When it comes to traits, you are looking for recruits with insight and, always, curiosity.

Insight

Insight is the innate ability to see the big picture, and it is vitally important in this phase, when leaders must look up from their initial hard work and out into the future. This is the landscape in which the sustainable company must ultimately survive and thrive. For insight in action, look back at Chapter Eight, where Mark Tercek shows us how to rise above the current noise and see how it leads us to concrete courses of action.

Curiosity

Although I place this trait in the third phase, curious people are vital at every stage of the sustainability transformation. Indeed, that is why Chapter Nine points to evidence of curiosity throughout the preceding stories of traits and competencies. But curiosity becomes ever more important along the way. It is not an idle game, but a theme that drives an organization toward new possibilities. To borrow from evolution, curiosity introduces variation, to which the culture can then apply selection. For this reason, a leader must pay special attention to ensure that curiosity is running strong in every phase of the journey.

Key Cultural Attribute

Openness

The critical cultural attribute for the third phase is openness. An organization that is open is one that can candidly assess its current situation and be open to the adaptations it may have to embrace in the future, as you saw in Chapter Twelve, demonstrated by Alberto Weisser's irreverent perspective about his company's business model. An open organization is receptive to ideas within its walls and beyond, partnerships inside its industry and out. It is unafraid and not threatened by change. Openness means acting authentically and in good faith with stakeholders. It means making an enemy of dogmatism and rigidity.

Cultural Pitfall

Gandhi said that no culture can live if it attempts to be exclusive. The cultural attribute of openness, so vitally important, points to the most dangerous pitfall of the third phase: tribalism. A culture that has tasted success in its pursuit of purpose runs the risk of getting too comfortable, too fat and happy, within its own walls. As the end of Chapter Twelve foreshadowed, a tribal culture can become "inbred" with its shared history and background. This is a tight culture that is in agreement on most if not all things. Decisions get made quickly, which looks like a good thing until you consider that all this agreeability may stem from a fundamental lack of diverse thinking. This is a culture that is susceptible to the "not invented here" school of resistance. The antidote to that, of course, is openness.

Building a culture of purpose is simple, but it's not easy. Along the way, the phases are meant to provide direction as you execute your own transformation. The figure on the next page illustrates the demarcation points to help gauge where you are in the journey, and what's next. And one of the biggest

Vernacular and Cultural Markers Serve as Demarcation Points

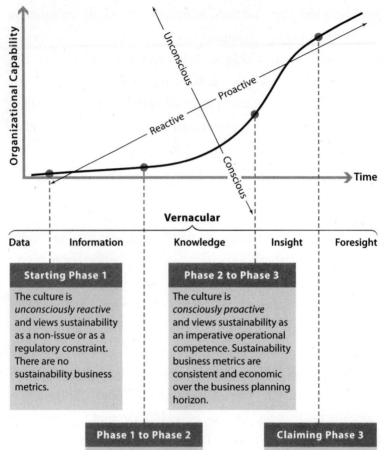

Starting Phase 1

The culture is *unconsciously reactive* and views sustainability as a non-issue or as a regulatory constraint. There are no sustainability business metrics.

Phase 2 to Phase 3

The culture is *consciously proactive* and views sustainability as an imperative operational competence. Sustainability business metrics are consistent and economic over the business planning horizon.

Phase 1 to Phase 2

The culture is *consciously reactive* and views sustainability as an unavoidable mandate. Sustainability business metrics are inconsistent or non-economic.

Claiming Phase 3

The culture is *unconsciously proactive* and views sustainability as a core value. Sustainability business metrics are economic over the very long term and reflective of the purpose.

challenges facing any leader is distraction. Even as the important work of creating a culture of purpose is under way, there will still be the ongoing challenges of running a profitable business. As you progress on sustainability, hundreds of things will seem more important at any given time. And if *you* don't see them, surely someone in your firm will try to use them to get your attention. "We can worry about culture stuff when the [insert crisis of the quarter] is over!" It will be difficult to maintain focus in those moments. The phases are here to act as your guideposts.

Three things are worth pointing out. First, this journey is not linear and monolithic throughout an organization. Parts of a company may be further along; particular initiatives may be lagging across an entire organization. Second, the building blocks described are cumulative. An organization making its way into the second phase does not substitute resilience for energy, but builds on energy with resilience.

Third, the middle part of this transformation, the *conscious* transition from *reactive* to *proactive*, is the hardest bit. The state of unawareness early in the journey can be quite comfortable, and I have yet to come across an organization that has developed into a culture of purpose that would trade that state for any other. But the middle of the journey requires gumption. But trust me: it's worth it.

Epilogue

If you build it, will it last?

Reflecting on your own organization and looking ahead, you might find yourself thinking not only about how to build a culture of purpose but also about how to maintain it.

The term "culture of purpose" might be new, but the idea predates the Anthropocene. In the fourteenth century, the philosopher Ibn Khaldun wrote about social cohesion among Berbers, noting that the desert tribespeople had more of it than settled societies. That social cohesion yielded courage, and it allowed the Berbers to conquer the lands of those who had become complacent. Having conquered them, the Berbers themselves drifted into complacency as their social cohesion frayed, ushering in the next dynasty. According to Khaldun, social cohesion arose spontaneously in tribal cultures, particularly those that had cause to want to change things—in other words, a purpose.

Throughout history, two conditions have caused cultures of purpose to wane: achieving their purpose or growing beyond the scale that can consistently contain it.

Each of these two conditions brings up a key question to take on your journey. Regarding the first, what has to be true about your purpose for it to be itself sustainable? There's a fine balance between being aspirational and being quixotic. On the one hand, the purpose must be more than a cakewalk destination beyond which the bonds between the people reaching for it will disintegrate. On the other hand, it cannot be so removed from reality that it fails to bond people together with a shared desire to achieve. The good news is that you have an actionable echo of your purpose in the quality of talent that flocks to you and stays with you: the people who make up your culture.

As for the second condition, is growth—for example, growth in revenues—a reasonable strategic metric for an organization? It's certainly an effective metric for a cancer, but individual cancers are not around for long if they are successful. To be clear: there is nothing wrong with growth per se, but it should be a by-product of doing the right things, rather than the aim of doing things right. It's a good servant, but a terrible master. The kind of growth that markets have historically liked best—say, a steady 5 percent every year—is destructive to a culture of purpose because its constancy makes it the master of the organization. But here, too, we find good news. The steady-growth mentality is gutted by what we now know about long-term value creation.[1] Adherence to purpose trumps delivery of invariant growth.

234

What emerges from history is that cultures of purpose, whether or not they endured, have been an integral part of humanity. And that means that they can be built here and today. This book is about the building blocks and the sequence in which to assemble them. And because all these building blocks can be selected or developed, you have the stuff to build your own culture of purpose. That's crucial; otherwise this book would simply be a juiced-up version of "Be brilliant!"

The cultures of purpose I have experienced were enabled by the traits and competencies of their people. But what strikes me first every time is the passion and intent of those people, the trust among them, and the conspicuous absence of cynicism. Indeed, a culture of purpose constantly bets on the passion of its people, and refuses, wherever possible, to accept the tyranny of "B players"[2] who lack that passion.

It's easy to be pessimistic about business when worker compensation languishes while executive pay continues to grow along with corporate profits. But ours is a time to be confident. We have learned that attracting top talent is becoming disproportionally challenging for companies with such growing disparities. We discovered in these pages an increasing number of organizations doing aspirational stuff with great people. Some are cultures of purposes, others are seeking their way. But in each instance, we found building blocks for such cultures. More than ever, top talent is gravitating to cultures of purpose. Sustainability is the most reliable path toward such cultures.

We have a road map for what's ahead. In the twenty-first century, businesses fueled by cultures of purpose will not only be profitable and among the best investments but also act as unmatched forces for good. Great leaders will be measured by their ability to marry purpose to profit. Some have begun already.

Will you join them?

Notes

Introduction

1. Edgar H. Schein, an organizational psychologist, offered a comprehensive interpretive definition of culture as "the accumulated shared learning of a given group, covering behavioral, emotional, and cognitive elements of the group members' total psychological functioning. For such learning to occur, there must be a history of shared experience that, in turn, implies some stability of membership in the group. Given such stability and a shared history, the human need for stability, consistency, and meaning will cause the various elements to form into patterns that eventually can be called a culture." Edgar H. Schein, *Organizational Culture and Leadership* (Hoboken, NJ: Wiley, 2006), 17.

2. Lyle M. Spencer Jr. and Signe M. Spencer, *Competence at Work* (Hoboken, NJ: Wiley, 1993).

3. Some have likened the emergence of sustainability to the Industrial Revolution, which itself had a profound effect on culture and socioeconomics by increasing the efficiency of commerce, just as radical transparency will. But the Industrial Revolution was a gradual process spanning a century, one that did not reach a tipping point but rather spread gradually across markets. And, unlike the rise of sustainability, the Industrial Revolution was driven by the privileged few. The masses, if they had a collective voice

at all, were represented by the followers of Ned Ludd, who mostly complained or else impetuously destroyed machinery.

4. John Mackey and Rajendra Sisodia, *Conscious Capitalism: Liberating the Heroic Spirit of Business* (Boston: Harvard Business Review Press, 2013).

5. Because sustainability is a way of traveling rather than a destination, for this book I chose organizations by how firmly they have committed to the journey rather than by whether they happen to be in the lead on any one dimension. My intent is not to claim all of these as fully wrought cultures of purpose, but to demonstrate that the building blocks of such cultures are ubiquitous and that most companies can embark on the journey to assemble them.

Chapter 1

1. This is consistent with the lessons of social psychology. Geert Hofstede showed how the values of a culture can be changed by changing behaviors and mental programs. Geert Hofstede, *Culture's Consequences: International Differences in Work-Related Values*, Cross-Cultural Research and Methodology Series (Thousand Oaks, CA: Sage), 5: 14–37.

2. Dacher Keltner, Deborah H. Gruenfeld, and Cameron Anderson, "Power, Approach, and Inhibition," *Psychological Review* 110, no. 2 (2003): 277.

Chapter 2

1. *Immunity to change*, a concept developed by Robert Kegan, is defined as "processes of dynamic equilibrium, which, like an immune system, powerfully and mysteriously tend to keep things pretty much as they are." Robert Kegan and Lisa Laskow Lahey, *How the Way We Talk Can Change the Way We Work: Seven Languages for Transformation* (San Francisco: Jossey-Bass, 2001), 5.

Chapter 3

1. Selective attention has been described in various settings, the most common being the cocktail party effect of tuning in on what the person in front of you says in a noisy room. An experiment viscerally expanding this effect from the auditory to the visual domain was conducted in 1999, when people who were asked to count passes among basketball players failed to notice a gorilla strolling across the court. Each of these settings shows how we can focus on a particular stimulus while filtering out a range of other

stimuli. Daniel J. Simons and Christopher F. Chabris, "Gorillas in Our Midst: Sustained Inattentional Blindness for Dynamic Events," *Perception* 28 (1999): 1059–1074.

2. EBITDA, short for Earnings Before Interest, Taxes, Depreciation and Amortization, is a dominant metric for the operational profitability of a business.

3. Lee Scott, "Twenty First Century Leadership" (October 23, 2005), http://news.walmart.com/executive-viewpoints/twenty-first-century-leadership.

4. Ran Kivetz, Oleg Urminsky, and Yuhuang Zheng, "The Goal-Gradient Hypothesis Resurrected: Purchase Acceleration, Illusionary Goal Progress, and Customer Retention," *Journal of Marketing Research* 43 (February 2006): 39–58.

Chapter 4

1. Will Gompertz, "Edvard Munch's Iconic Artwork The Scream Sold for $120m," *BBC News* (May 3, 2012), http://www.bbc.co.uk/news/entertainment-arts-17926519.

2. Kelly Crow, "The Auctioneer Holds Forth on Money, Desire and the State of the Art," *Wall Street Journal*, March 24, 2011, http://on.wsj.com/1fRdXbl.

3. Graham Bowley, "Principal Auctioneer of Sotheby's Is Leaving Post," *New York Times*, November 22, 2103, http://www.nyti.ms/1aEfG1P.

4. Michael R. Bloomberg, *Bloomberg by Bloomberg* (Hoboken, NJ: Wiley, 1997).

5. Indeed, intrinsic motivation can correlate inversely to material rewards, as was demonstrated in Edward L. Deci, Richard Koestner, and Richard M. Ryan, "A Meta-Analytic Review of Experiments Examining the Effects of Extrinsic Rewards on Intrinsic Motivation," *Psychological Bulletin* 125, no. 6 (November 1999): 626–668.

6. Christopher Marquis, Daniel Beunza, Fabrizio Ferraro, and Bobbi Thomason, "Driving Sustainability at Bloomberg L.P.," Harvard Business Review case study (August 13, 2010). Available at Harvard Business Review, prod. no. 411025-PDF-ENG, http://hbr.org/product/driving-sustainability-at-bloomberg-l-p/an/411025-PDF-ENG.

7. ESG data captures environmental, social, and corporate governance domains. It is the bare-knuckled doppelgänger of "sustainability data," which to many financial analysts sounds too fluffy.

Chapter 5

1. Johanna Mair and Mark Fruechtnicht, "A Puma vs. Giants: The Rise of David," IESE case study (September 10, 2007). Available at Harvard Business Review, prod. no. IES220-PDF-ENG, http://hbr.org/product /a-puma-vs-giants-the-rise-of-david/an/IES220-PDF-ENG.
2. Emma Jacobs, "On Philosophers and Profits," *Financial Times*, May 29, 2011, http://on.ft.com/THj6u5.
3. "PPR Becomes Kering," PPR press release, Kering, March 22, 2013, http://www.kering.com/en/press-releases/ppr_becomes_kering.
4. Streufert Satish, "Strategic Management Simulations to Prepare for VUCAD Terrorism," *Journal of Homeland Security*, June 23, 2006.

Chapter 6

1. Gregory S. Berns, Samuel M. McClure, Giuseppe Pagnoni, and P. Read Montague, "Predictability Modulates Human Brain Response to Reward," *Journal of Neuroscience* 21, no. 8 (April 15, 2001): 2793–2798. To see how fun can change behavior, see TheFunTheory's video on piano stairs, which increased by two-thirds the number of people who used stairs rather than the escalator: "Piano stairs - TheFunTheory.com - Rolighetsteorin.se," YouTube (October 7, 2009), http://www.youtu.be /2lXh2n0aPyw.
2. Coined by Daniel Goleman, the term *amygdala hijack* denotes an emotional and irrational response that is significantly disproportionate to its stimulus. Daniel Goleman, *Emotional Intelligence: Why It Can Matter More Than IQ* (New York:Bantam Books, 1996).

Chapter 7

1. In the Stanford Marshmallow Test, conducted by psychologist Walter Mischel in the 1960s and 1970s, children between the ages of three and five were offered a choice between a marshmallow provided immediately or two marshmallows later if they waited until the experimenter returned a short period later. Following these subjects through life over the coming decades, researchers found that children who were able to wait longer (in other words, to delay gratification) had better life outcomes on average on multiple quantifiable metrics. Yuichi Shoda, Walter Mischel, and Philip K. Peake, "Predicting Adolescent Cognitive and Self-Regulatory Competencies from Preschool Delay of Gratification:

Identifying Diagnostic Conditions," *Developmental Psychology* 26, no. 6 (1990): 978–986.

Chapter 8

1. Fluid intelligence, which includes both inductive and deductive reasoning, is the capacity to think logically through situations beyond one's body of previously acquired knowledge. It expands one's acquired knowledge with new patterns and relationships using abstraction and synthesis. For more on fluid intelligence, see Raymond B. Cattell, "Theory of Fluid and Crystallized Intelligence: A Critical Experiment," *Journal of Educational Psychology* 54 (1963): 1–22.

Chapter 9

1. Curiosity thrives in the presence of accidents and failure, and is itself the engine for creativity, as psychologist Todd Kashdan has shown. Educators are taking notice. An increasing number of universities that offer undergraduate and graduate degrees focused on creativity explicitly embrace the notion of failure. At Penn State, for instance, Professor Jack Matson tellingly refers to his course "Creativity, Innovation and Change" as "Failure 101." Todd Kashdan, *Curious? Discover the Missing Ingredient to a Fulfilling Life* (New York: William Morrow, 2009).
2. Lee D. Ross, "The Intuitive Psychologist and His Shortcomings," in *Advances in Experimental Social Psychology*, ed. Leonard Berkowitz (New York: Academic Press, 1977), 10: 174–214.
3. Kent C. Berridge and Terry E. Robinson, "What Is the Role of Dopamine in Reward: Hedonic Impact, Reward Learning, or Incentive Salience?" *Brain Research Reviews* 28, no. 3 (December 1998): 309–369.

Part 3

1. Craig Haney, Curtis Banks, and Philip Zimbardo, "A Study of Prisoners and Guards in a Simulated Prison," *Naval Research Reviews* (September 1973).

Chapter 10

1. Psychologist Mihály Csíkszentmihályi defines flow as the mental state experienced when performing a task at a high level with energy, engagement, and joy. Mihály Csíkszentmihályi, *Flow: The Psychology of Optimal Experience* (New York: Harper & Row, 1990).

2. "Christoph Lueneburger Interviews Yvon Chouinard," YouTube (April 21, 2012), http://youtu.be/5nZcPTXQ9Ig.
3. For more on this experiment by social psychologist Muzafer Sherif, known as the Robbers Cave Study, see Bernard E. Whitley Jr. and Mary E. Kite, *The Psychology of Prejudice and Discrimination* (Belmont, CA: Wadsworth, 2010), 326–327.
4. The term *collective effervescence* was first mentioned by the French sociologist Émile Durkheim, who wrote about settings in which people "believe themselves to be transported into an entirely different world from the one they have before their eyes." Émile Durkheim, *The Elementary Forms of the Religious Life*, trans. J. W. Swain (London: George Allen & Unwin, 1915), 214–226.
5. LBOs, or leveraged buy-outs, were characteristic of KKR's investment style. Initially referred to as "bootstrap" deals by the firms' founders, LBOs use significant debt to finance the acquisition of controlling stakes in companies like Borden.

Chapter 11

1. Crossnore has about one hundred students, intentionally below the maximum number of people with whom one can maintain stable social relationships, which anthropologist Robin Dunbar pegged at about 150 people. Dunbar's number was borne out by his anthropological and ethnographical research, which found that tribes and villages throughout human history split when the number of members exceeded the range of one hundred to two hundred. For more information, see R.I.M. Dunbar, "Coevolution of Neocortical Size, Group Size and Language in Humans," *Behavioral and Brain Sciences* 16, no. 4 (1993): 681–735.
2. Jean Piaget, *The Psychology of Intelligence*, trans. Malcolm Piercy and D. E. Berlyne (London: Routledge & Kegan Paul, 1950).

Chapter 12

1. Stanley Milgram, "Behavioral Study of Obedience," *Journal of Abnormal and Social Psychology* 67, no. 4 (1963): 371–378.
2. The term *black team* originates with IBM, which in the 1960s had an army of software testing specialists. Noticing that some of these people were up to 20 percent faster than their peers, IBM assembled the best ones into a separate team. Suddenly, the people with a real passion for finding software bugs were entirely among themselves. The team soon began to look

different (think handlebar mustaches), and in reference to the black attire its members favored, the group came to be known as "the black team." They were respected for their ability to find and fix bugs, and if you were a programmer at IBM, you did not want the black team unleashed on your work. By unflinchingly getting to the root of software problems, IBM's black team had a significant impact on the quality of the company's code.

Chapter 13

1. Christoph Lueneburger and Daniel Goleman, "The Change Leadership Sustainability Demands," *Sloan Management Review* 51, no. 4 (2010): 49–55.
2. David Dunning, Kerri Johnson, Joyce Ehrlinger, and Justin Kruger, "Why People Fail to Recognize Their Own Incompetence," *Current Directions in Psychological Science* 12, no. 3 (2003): 83–87.

Epilogue

1. Edward Hess, *Smart Growth: Building an Enduring Business by Managing the Risks of Growth* (New York: Columbia University Press, 2010).
2. The tyranny of B players describes the organizational reluctance, usually rooted in a fear of perceived disruption and uncertainty, to change people who are not playing to their strengths. Experience tells us that settling for "good enough" is rarely the optimal route, although always the one that takes less effort. Not only that, we also risk denying some B players the chance to become A players in other roles.

Acknowledgments

When my father was in jail, I was not allowed to visit him, so instead he wrote letters. In each of them, he asked what I was learning. This question has stayed with me, and without it I would not have written this book. Thank you, Klaus.

Having written this book, I know that it would have been about as engaging as knitting instructions without all the people who appear in these pages and graciously shared their stories. I am grateful to each of them.

Much of what I have learned about cultures of purpose originated in the work of the Sustainability Practice of Egon Zehnder. I am immensely grateful to all its members and two colleagues in particular: Richard Murray-Bruce, who was there from the beginning and proved instrumental not only in finding answers but in figuring out what questions we should be asking. And Carrie Ngo, whose dogged leadership of research helped build the Sustainability Practice into a market leader.

Then there were those who inspired me to sit down and write. To Dan Goleman, with whom I had the privilege of publishing in MIT's *Sloan Management Review*: thank you for your wisdom, encouragement, and Foreword. To Claudio Fernández-Aráoz, who blazed a trail wide enough for me to follow: thank you for unfailingly meeting my questions with insight and patience. To my partners Damien O'Brien and Alan Hilliker, who saw value in the message of this book: thank you for giving me the freedom to pursue it.

I am also grateful to the Aspen Institute for giving wings to this project and introducing me to other fellows who accelerated my thinking. In particular, I thank Josh Henretig, Meg Siegal, Abe Tarapani, and Kristian Villumsen.

Leah Spiro helped find the right home for this book and rolled her eyes much less often than I gave her occasion to do. Karen Murphy forced me to be clear, not only until I was frustrated but until I understood what I was trying to say. To Ellen Neuborne, Michele Jones, Mary Garrett, and Jackie O'Sullivan: thank you for your tireless edits and suggestions—and for tolerating my stubbornness. Steve Kelner and Melinda Merino deftly lent precision and context to my thinking. I owe much to my assistant Mark Nieves, who kept the trains running on time; to Elena Dowling and Verena Renze-Westendorf, who gave me insight instead of data; and to Renu Grover, who kept on finding truffles. Paula Patterson and the little man in her belly kept me in good stead with illustrative brilliance and wit.

Many helped me connect with people who appear in these pages—chief among them José Calderón, Luis Garreaud, Neil Hawkins, German Herrera, Martha Josephson,

Brent Magnuson, Bill Massa, Justus O'Brien, Brian Reinken, Jonathan Rose, Gabriel Sánchez-Zinny, Jeff Seabright, and Erik Slingerland.

Some of the questions that most tested my thinking came over a bottle of wine or two, and I toast David Noble, Douglas Choo, and Dief N. Baker; Rick and Jennifer Ridgeway; Mr. Mece d/b/a Sandro Di Fusco; and the effervescent folks at North of Neutral.

A shout-out to my mates Erik Becker, Francisco Paret, Joseph Gravier, and Bruce Chase. Erik: your thinking about culture, even capernoited at Chungking Mansions, was spot-on. Paco: your aversion to bullshit steered me toward clarity. Joe: you kept my brain oxygenated. One day I'll keep up with you. Bruce: you're crazy, mate.

There were countless moments of inspiration, and I especially thank David Blood, Gro Brundtland, Willy Burkhardt, Audrey Choi, Yvon Chouinard, Al Gore, Jason Jay, Kim Jeffery, Jakob Kaschper, Dambisa Moyo, John Ruggie, and Richard Sarnoff.

And finally, my family. To my wife, Anne, who didn't yet know me when she took a left turn toward Paris with me on a Sunday afternoon: let's keep turning left—I love the wild and wonderful ride with you. I am deeply grateful for you and our daughter, Liv. Thank you both for putting up with me as I worked on this book. Let's play!

About the Author

Christoph Lueneburger is a partner at Egon Zehnder, a global leader in leadership strategy services, board consulting, and executive search. A fluid dynamicist and former private equity investor, he founded the firm's Sustainability Practice, which grew to a market-leading position under his leadership. Christoph now heads the firm's global private equity practice.

Christoph's career started in the specialty materials sector, where he holds multiple patents and rose to run a European manufacturer. Transitioning to private equity, he then focused on deals in the water sector. He began to think begrudgingly about sustainability while carrying cases of imported sparkling water to the fourth-story flat of his then-fiancée in Paris.

Venturing beyond the intersection of value creation and talent, Christoph has designed and built a game-changing rowing shell and also imagines himself to be the only person to have traversed Alaska's Mt. McKinley and Timbuktu's Niger Valley within the same month. At the top of his bucket list is riding the Pan-American Highway by motorcycle.

Christoph has lived and worked in the United States, Canada, France, and Germany and is a fellow at the Aspen Institute. He now resides in New York with his wife and daughter.

For more information, please visit egonzehnder.com and cultureofpurpose.com.

Index

Strategic orientation competency: description of, 82–83; how Jochen Zeitz giving sustainability to PUMA using his, 85–93; markers for the, 93–95; Mitch Seavey winning the Iditarod sled dog race (2013), 81–82; Phase Three: the advanced phase, 227; red flags indicating the opposite of, 95; required for culture of purpose, 3; three fundamentally integrated components of, 83; transformational nature of, 84–85

Sustainability: using authority and veto power to drive, 39–41; change leadership as critical competency for transformation, 16; as cultural of purpose characteristic, 1–2; Curtis Ravenel's ability to drive Bloomberg toward, 67–79; demystifying how it affects value, 72; engagement in order to move toward, 104–115; examining the "who" and the "where" of, 7; framed as a compelling story, 37; historical parallel between fall of communism and need for, 8–9; how a resilience attribute is critical to process of, 185–190; how Andy Ruben moved Walmart toward, 50–61; how Frank O'Brien-Bernini boosted Owens Corning's, 16–24, 26; how it was brought to Lend Lease through Pascal Mittermaier's influence, 34–43; how Jochen Zeitz gave PUMA, 85–93, 154–155; Kees Kruythoff on providing consumers a better life through, 191; Peter Bakker's determination driving TNT's, 123–133; redefined at Chrysler, 180–181; the results delivery competency as driver toward, 47–50; siloed thinking on topic of, 38; Unilever's public forum on, 191–192. See also Environmental protection

Sustainability journey: additional thoughts on, 231; organizational capability over the course of, 218, 230; Phase One: the early stage, 218, 219–223, 230; Phase Two: the intermediate phase, 131, 223–226, 230; Phase Three: the advanced phase, 218, 226–229, 230; purpose condition required for a successful, 234; reasonable growth condition for a successful, 234; the starting point for, 217, 219. See also Cultures of purpose

Sustainability Practice (Egon Zehnder), 2, 217

T

Takács, Károly, 36–37

"Taking Ownership" initiative (Borden Group), 176

Talent: gravitating to cultures of purpose, 236; markers for curiosity trait, 162–163; markers for determination trait, 133–134; markers for the engagement trait, 115–117; markers for the insight trait, 148–150; recognizing and seeking out specific traits in new, 97–98

Tercek, Mark: early willingness to take opportunities, 140–141, 142; environmental business while at Goldman Sachs, 143–144, 148; his career trajectory marked by his curiosity, 157–158; insight on benefits of freely sharing credit, 141–142; insight to change his leadership style at TNC, 147; lifelong use of insight by, 139–140, 228; as TNC (The Nature Conservancy) head, 144–147, 158

TNC (The Nature Conservancy): Mark Tercek's insight to change leadership style at, 147; Mark Tercek's position as head of, 144–146, 158;